How to
WIN
with High
Self-Esteem

How to
WIN
with High
Self-Esteem

MACK R. DOUGLAS

Foreword by
Phyllis Beaver
Wayne A. Nagy
Robert Wolgamott

PELICAN PUBLISHING COMPANY
Gretna 1994

*The word "Pelican" and the depiction of a pelican are
trademarks of Pelican Publishing Company, Inc., and are
registered in the U.S. patent and trademark office.*

Library of Congress Cataloging-in-Publication Data

Douglas, Mack R.
   How to win with high self-esteem / Mack R. Douglas.
     p.   cm.
   Includes bibliographic references.
   ISBN 0-88289-994-5
   1. Self-esteem. 2. Success—Psychological aspects. I. Title.
BF697.5.S46D68   1994
158′.1—dc20   93-5874
                                           CIP

All Scripture quotations are taken from *The Scofield Reference
Bible: The Holy Bible, Authorized King James Version.* Copyright ©
1917 by Oxford University Press.

Manufactured in the United States of America
Published by Pelican Publishing Company, Inc.
1101 Monroe Street, Gretna, Louisiana 70053

To Mary, my wife, whose undying support of me is fantastic.

To Claire, Don, Laura, Elaine, their mates, and children, who affirm me constantly.

To Dr. Bob Wolgamott, whose clients in Portland, Oregon, and Tucson, Arizona, call him blessed—for his friendship and foreword.

To Wayne Nagy, an outstanding motivational speaker and the most effective high school principal I've ever known—for his foreword.

To Dr. Phyllis Beaver, whose unexcelled skills in instructional design led Florida Power and Light Company, the only non-Japanese company to receive the Deming Award for Corporate Excellence—for her dear friendship and foreword.

To Mary Kaye Bates, whose styling and final editing put the icing on this manuscript.

And to you, the reader: enjoy the new person you are destined to become.

Contents

Foreword

Mack R. Douglas has spent his entire life helping others to bring out the best in themselves. This is a gift that has brought him a life of great joy and satisfaction. Now he has cleverly crafted a book in which he passes on his gift to us if we simply follow through on each of his pages of wisdom.

In a refreshing literary approach, Mack teaches us how to improve our own self-esteem as well as of those around us. His sparkling wit and vividly described personal experiences provide the perfect background for the easy-to-follow exercises throughout the book.

Although the author has written this book simply to help each of us enhance our own self-esteem, it can be used for so many other applications. It is a wonderful treasure chest of material for any college professor to use with students who are studying in the fields of nursing, human resources, education, and psychology. Teachers for kindergarten through twelfth grade will also find it a helpful tool and, of course, parents will find it invaluable in guiding and nurturing their children.

How lucky you are to have found this book. It will change your life.

PHYLLIS BEAVER, PH.D.

As a practicing educator I am keenly aware of the need for children to develop high self-esteem. Over the past ten years I have had the privilege of being a principal of an inner-city junior high, a suburban middle school, and a culturally diverse high school. In each situation, regardless of race, ethnic background, gender, or socio-economic status, the successful students had one thing in common: *high self-esteem*.

Since education is a family affair, we are all responsible for understanding the importance of self-esteem in our own lives so that we may better prepare our children for a successful, rewarding life.

Thanks to Dr. Mack Douglas, we now have the tool to understand and put into practice the principles of life and to teach our children these important principles.

I highly recommend this book as required reading for those individuals who choose to lead a fulfilling life and to those who choose to enrich the lives of our children.

WAYNE A. NAGY
High School Principal
Past President: Florida Association
of School Administrators

There is an old proverb that states, "As a man thinketh, so is he." Negative self-esteem or negative thinking that always focuses on one's inadequacies contributes to the image that one is less than others. This, in turn, breeds negative emotions such as sadness, anger, frustration, envy, jealousy, and fear. All of these have destructive elements that may create mental depression. Internalized anger and other emotions contribute to an over-utilization of neurohormones of the brain such as serotonin and norepinephrine. The net result of mental depression is physical depression, which in turn contributes to the development of physical illnesses such as headaches, stomach ulcers, spastic colon, and other emotionally related conditions.

During the more than twenty years that I have known Dr. Mack Douglas, I have been impressed with his ability to recognize that taking on the role of the victim is detrimental to both mental and physical health. Victimization affects one's self-esteem, one's marriage, one's standing in the community, one's ability to relate to society at large, and in one's ability to move forward in an upwardly mobile fashion to provide for his family and their needs. In this, his latest book, this dedicated author has gone to great lengths to develop a workbook that, if read, reread, and used correctly, will help turn lives around. By applying the principles outlined in this material, people no longer need to be victims, but can feel better about themselves. They find they can enjoy higher regard from their families and friends. Their role in society can be successful and satisfying.

Dr. Douglas has laid out step-by-step guidelines and principles that, if judiciously followed and put into practice, are guaranteed to make a major difference in your life. Initially, he helps you understand what self-esteem is. He then discusses how you should go about dealing with yourself, breaking the habit of being victimized by yourself and others. Next, he takes you through the steps necessary to rewrite a new vision for your life. Again, there is an old proverb that says, "Where there is no vision, the people perish." It is important that each individual break the habit of being the victim by taking control of his own life, developing a vision for the future, and in that way begin to rebuild his life. It is a reasonably well known fact that if a person is going to build a house, he must first visualize it in his mind. The plans or blueprints are next drawn, adding the distinguishing features all prior to building the house. Nearly every significant thing in the world was first someone else's vision. The San Francisco Bay Bridge was first a vision long before plans were drawn or it was finally built. In a similar manner, it is necessary for us to visualize what we wish to do with our lives. We need to begin to make the necessary short-term, intermediate, and long-term plans toward this goal. Dr. Douglas points the way to carry out this planning on a level for the physical world in which we live as well as for the relationships we enjoy or wish to enjoy.

Dr. Douglas further understands and writes well on the successful life in which the mental, physical, and spiritual realms are integrated and balanced to make man whole.

I enthusiastically recommend the steps in this book be put into practice for a successful life. I commend Dr. Douglas on his careful coordination of material for your benefit.

ROBERT C. WOLGAMOTT, M.D., FAPA
Board Certified Psychiatrist

Introduction

Thomas A. Edison said that the greatest gift parents can give to their children is enthusiasm.

The foundation of enthusiasm is high self-esteem—*that package of beliefs you carry around in your head that you have accepted to be the truth about yourself whether it is or not.*

To the person with high self-esteem this book is an inspiration to maintain that value.

To the person with low self-esteem this book can be your journey to high self-esteem. Like all journeys, it isn't always easy. There will be detours and roadblocks, and you may never totally reach your destination. But the journey will bring you the highest and most joyous experiences of your life. In order to get the most from your journey:

1. Make a commitment to yourself that you deserve high self-esteem.
2. Daily experience the conduct and activity necessary to take charge of and change your life.

Your endorphins will produce for you the most wonderful feelings you have ever known.

You are worth it!

How to
WIN
with High
Self-Esteem

CHAPTER 1

What Is Self-Esteem?

Esteem is defined as *appreciation, worth, estimate of value.* *Self-esteem* is the package of beliefs that you carry around in your head, that you have accepted to be the truth about yourself, whether it is or not.

His mother was a forceful, domineering woman incapable of giving love to her son. Married three times, she was divorced by her second husband because she beat him up regularly. His father died before he was born, and his mother had to work long hours to survive.

She gave him no affection, no discipline, and no training. He was alone and rejected by his mother and other children. He was ugly, poor, untrained, and unloved. At age 13, he was told by a school psychologist that he didn't know the meaning of the word *love*.

Although he had a high IQ, he failed repeatedly in school and quit during his third year of high school.

He joined the Marine Corps, but he rebelled against authority, was court-martialed, and received an undesirable discharge.

He moved to a foreign country and married a woman who was an illegitimate child and who bore him two children. She fought him, bullied him, and locked him in the bathroom. After she kicked him out, he crawled back and begged her for another chance.

She ridiculed his failure and even made fun of his sexual impotency in front of a friend. He felt utterly rejected.

On November 22, 1963, he shot and killed Pres. John F. Kennedy. His name was Lee Harvey Oswald.

Born into a prominent, wealthy family with a strong mother, this person was told from birth that he was destined to be president of the United States. He had for his role model a cousin who was considered one of the greatest achievers of his day and a very popular international figure.

Handsome, cultured, well-educated, he early excelled in politics. Then, at the height of his early success, he was struck down by a devastating illness that would have left most everyone else a mental and emotional cripple.

Not him. He was destined for greater things. He went on to become president of the United States, saved his nation from its worst financial depression, and led his country victoriously through its most far-flung war. His name was Franklin Delano Roosevelt.

Two examples of self-esteem: one of low self-esteem, one of high self-esteem.

Everything you do is determined by your value judgment of yourself.

Commitment. "The quality of a person's life is determined by his commitment to excellence." (Vince Lombardi)

People with high self-esteem can and do make a commitment to a cause that's equal to or greater than themselves. Make your motto "The greatest use of life is to so live your life that the use of your life outlives your life."

People with low self-esteem cannot make a commitment to anything. They are filled with fear, doubt, and anxiety.

Relationships. We must love people and use things, not love things and use people.

All child abusers were themselves abused as children.

One hundred percent of hard-core drug abusers have low self-esteem.

"It's no exaggeration to say that a strong, positive self-image is the best possible preparation for success in life."
Dr. Joyce Brothers

The fatal attraction syndrome (developed in detail in a later chapter) is a prime example of low self-esteem. When this person fails to receive the high emotions he expected in passionate love, he starts to control and manipulate his/her partner because he fears that person will leave. When that person leaves, the victim fears the loss of not only the promised savior, but also fears a loss of himself. That's when violent action results.

One summer at church youth camp, we invited several teens from a children's home to be our guests. Gordon Minyard, sixteen years old, was two years behind in school and so filled with low self-esteem he kept his head buried between his shoulders.

My wife and I invited Gordon to move into our home as a foster child. I will never forget the day I took him to the store and helped him choose his first suit, overcoat, and dress shoes. He was thrilled. We invested several hours each night guiding him in his studies. He went out for the junior high football team and quickly became a star. Each day he raised his head a bit more until within three months he stood proud and erect. His grades were *A*'s and *B*'s. He had his first case of "puppy love." In fact, the girls called him.

What happened? Gordon needed and received a home with role models that cared for him, showed him how to achieve, and made him responsible for his actions. In the classroom, on the football field, and in social relationships, he developed high self-esteem.

Emotional Conduct of Those with Low Self-Esteem	vs.	**Emotional Conduct of Those with High Self-Esteem**
1. Critical of others		1. Accepts others as they are
2. Pessimistic		2. Optimistic

Be kind, compassionate, and gentle with yourself.

3. Complains about circumstances

3. Looks at circumstances with acceptance

4. Short temper

4. Seldom loses temper; slow to anger

5. Never enough money, time, etc.

5. Plans life positively around money and time

6. Rejects help from others

6. Does not ask for help, but welcomes it

7. Expects perfection in self and others

7. Expects things to go well without demands

8. Carries heavy guilt

8. Loads no guilt on self or others

9. Unloads guilt on others as control

9. Never uses guilt as control

10. Tries to manipulate others

10. Never manipulates; does persuade

11. Usually overly dependent on God

11. Believes God expects us to act responsibly

12. Has rigid rules of conduct

12. Rules of conduct are flexible within reason

13. May be devoid of character

13. Has developed reasonable character guidelines

14. Easily addicted to alcohol, drugs, job, love, or religion

14. Has control over impulses; has own inner highs that are self-generated

A Self-Esteem Evaluation Exercise

(Pick those that best apply to you.)

CONDUCT

1. My conduct is usually beyond reproach.   no
2. When I get in trouble with others, it's usually not my fault.   no

---

If you don't prize yourself, who will? If you don't think well of yourself, why would anyone else?

3. I usually can influence others to do that which benefits both of us. *yes* +1
4. I cause trouble with my family members. *No*
5. I am good at the things I do at work, home, etc. *NO*
6. I never measure up to what I really want to be or do. *yes*
7. I treat other people in a way so that they feel important and of value. *yes*
8. My family and some of my friends are disappointed in me. *No*
9. I am basically a good person. *yes*
10. I can really be mean to other people. *yes*

MENTAL ACHIEVEMENTS

1. I am smart. *yes*
2. When I reach my goals, I will be known as an important person. *No*
3. I am well-behaved in all the things I do. *No*
4. I am an important and valued member of my family. *yes*
5. Other people at work, school, or home think I am smart and interesting. *yes*
6. I have trouble remembering things. *yes*
7. I have never used but a small fraction of my mental capabilities. *No*
8. I am dumb about things other than the very small world I live in daily. *No*
9. I would fear having to converse with someone with a good education. *No*
10. I really am not very smart. *No*

PHYSICAL APPEARANCE

1. My looks never please me. *No*
2. I am strong. *yes*
3. I can never get my hair the way I want it. *No*
4. I really am good-looking. *No*

Concentrate totally on what you want to accomplish.
In time, it will be yours.

5. Nothing in my wardrobe suits me.
6. I am popular with most everybody I meet.
7. I do not feel like my figure is as acceptable as I want it to be.
8. I do have beautiful eyes.
9. No one ever compliments me about my looks.
10. I am improving in strength and looks.

FEARS

1. I am often sad and unhappy.
2. My looks bother me.
3. I really worry a lot.
4. I am often afraid.
5. Little things worry me.
6. I face my problems and overcome them.
7. I have learned that the things you worry about never happen anyway. So I don't worry.
8. Fear is a coward. When you face it with facts and action, fear flees.
9. I have learned that I can be happy by expecting to feel happy.
10. I put joy and happiness in my life by doing the things that make me feel happy.

GETTING ALONG WITH OTHER PEOPLE

1. I feel other people are making fun of me behind my back.
2. It's hard for me to make new friends.
3. I am quite popular, because I care about people.
4. If you feel good about yourself, you will treat other people the same way.
5. I feel left out of things.
6. People often pick on me.
7. I have many friends and enjoy their companionship.

"When you have a lemon, make a lemonade."

Julius Rosenwald

8. My fellow workers or classmates include me in their conversation and activities. *yes*
9. I don't know how to meet new people and it's not pleasant. *no*
10. I am one of the most accepted and popular people I know. *no*

HAPPINESS

1. I am a happy person. *no*
2. I live a cheerful life. *no*
3. I wish things were different for me. *no*
4. Most other people I know are unhappy also. *yes*
5. I really like the life I live. *yes*
6. My family life is the greatest. *yes*
7. I am unhappy most of the time. *no*
8. Life really is the pits. *no*
9. I am easy to get along with. *yes*
10. Most days I'm sorry I got up. *no*

Answers to Self-Esteem Evaluation Exercise

Positive answers receive a +1; negative answers receive a −1.

CONDUCT: 1, 3, 5, 7, and 9 are positive statements; 2, 4, 6, 8, and 10 are negative statements.

MENTAL ACHIEVEMENTS: 1, 2, 3, 4, and 5 are positive; 6, 7, 8, 9, and 10 are negative.

PHYSICAL ACHIEVEMENTS: 2, 4, 6, 8, and 10 are positive; 1, 3, 5, 7, and 9 are negative.

FEARS: 6, 7, 8, 9, and 10 are positive; 1, 2, 3, 4, and 5 are negative.

GETTING ALONG WITH PEOPLE: 3, 4, 7, 8, and 10 are positive; 1, 2, 5, 6, and 9 are negative.

The road to success is always under construction.

HAPPINESS: 1, 2, 5, 6, and 9 are positive; 3, 4, 7, 8, and 10 are negative.

Scoring for Self-Esteem Exercise

30—50 +'s	super, confident, high self-esteem
10—29 —'s	well-defined high self-esteem
1—9 +'s	a shade more high self-esteem than low self-esteem
1—9 —'s	low self-esteem greater than high self-esteem
10—29 —'s	you really don't like yourself; work to change this attitude
30—50 —'s	you have a serious condition of low self-esteem; see a counselor for growth

Some years ago, a twenty-three-year-old pianist in a dance band in Los Angeles was on his way home from a gig at 2:30 A.M. On the freeway, he noticed a black lady standing beside her Mercedes frantically waving. He pulled over and she said, "My husband is dying of cancer in St. John's Hospital in Santa Monica. He has been in a coma and I was sent home at midnight for a bit of rest. I just received word he is alert and is calling for me. My car broke down. Will you take me to the hospital?"

He agreed and went some six miles out of his way. On the way over, she found out he wanted to become a concert pianist, but didn't have a piano at home to practice. She got his address.

Upon arriving at the hospital she offered him one hundred dollars for his trouble, but he wouldn't take it. She thanked him with deep appreciation.

Ten days later, they delivered to his apartment a $10,000 baby grand piano with this message: "You gave my husband and I twenty minutes together before he died of lung cancer. He also was a musician. We both wanted you to have this

---

There is nothing I cannot do if I want it badly enough.

piano in appreciation of those twenty minutes, and in encouragement of your music career." Mrs. Nat "King" (Maria) Cole.

He wouldn't have gone out of his way to take her to the hospital and she and her husband wouldn't have given him the piano if they didn't have high self-esteem.

The following statements will go a long way toward building your high self-esteem. Quote and live by one each day. The life you save will be your own.

Positive Self-Action Statements to Enhance My Self-Esteem

1. I am my final authority for everything I do.
2. I accept full responsibility for all my actions.
3. I allow myself the freedom to make mistakes.
4. I make my own decisions and willingly accept the consequences.
5. I think for myself and speak and act with deliberation.
6. I stand up for my own opinions and convictions.
7. I do not vacillate—I make the best choice I can at the time.
8. I do not accept condemnation, "put-downs," or insults.
9. I do not condemn or belittle myself for my mistakes and shortcomings.
10. I do not blame others for my problems, mistakes, defeats, or handicaps.
11. I do not lean on others for unjustified financial or moral support.
12. I take deep satisfaction in doing my work conscientiously and well.
13. I face reality and resist nothing I cannot change.
14. I refuse to accept any condemnation, blame, shame, or guilt.

Purpose is the engine that drives your life.

15. I refrain from no endeavor out of fear of unsatisfactory results.
16. I do not procrastinate; I do first things first.
17. I give precedence to my own needs and desires as I see fit.
18. I accept every problem and goal as a challenge to my awareness.
19. I purge myself of any blame, shame, guilt, or remorse.
20. I do not depend on others for confirmation or approval.
21. I do not accept advice against my better judgment.
22. I am patient, kind, and gentle with myself.
23. I discipline myself in line with my life objectives.
24. I do nothing to excess—I avoid self-indulgence.
25. I fulfill all commitments, both to myself and others.
26. I follow all undertakings through to a logical conclusion.
27. I follow all undertakings through to emotional satisfaction.
28. I take the initiative in personal contacts and relationships.
29. I freely express any emotion I see fit.
30. I readily admit my mistakes and shortcomings.
31. I walk erect and look everyone in the eye with a friendly gaze.
32. I do not deny my needs, feelings, or opinions to please others.
33. I am warm and friendly toward all I contact.
34. I recognize everyone as innately "good."
35. I feel warm and loving toward myself.
36. I am authentic, true to my own needs, values, and convictions.
37. I defer to no one on account of his wealth, power, or prestige.

"Be yourself. Who else is better qualified?"
Frank S. Giblin II

38. I count my blessings and rejoice in my growing awareness.

Conclusion

Love yourself. This may be a lifelong journey. If you didn't receive permission from your parents to love yourself, then give yourself permission to do so. Nineteen times in the Bible we are commanded to love ourselves. The apostle Paul writes: "So ought men to love their wives as their own bodies. He that loveth his wife loveth himself." (Eph. 5:28) After declaring that a man should love the Lord God with his whole heart, soul, mind, and strength, Jesus says, referring to the second of the two greatest commandments: "And the second is like, namely this, 'Thou shalt love thy neighbour as thyself.' There is none other greater commandment greater than these." (Mark 12:31) You now have biblical permission to love yourself. Do it.

Free your emotions. Experience joy, peace, happiness, elation, love, etc. Learn to enjoy these positive emotions. We learn by doing.

Give love to everyone else. Look for the good in everyone you meet; ignore those things you may not admire. Do something kind, positive, and gracious to others. Train yourself to always say "thank you" for every service rendered, even if it's to the person who holds the door for you at the mall. Write letters of appreciation. Give praise for good work done to those who work with you and especially for those who report to you. You'll be thrilled at the love that is returned.

"Once your mind is stretched to a new idea it will never again return to its original size."
Oliver Wendell Holmes

CHAPTER 2

How We Got This Way

Psychologist Carl Rogers said, "God gave children to parents expecting them to be raised as princes and princesses, but parents have turned many of them into frogs."

Eleanor Roosevelt said, "I craved attention all through my childhood, because I was made to feel so conscious of the fact that nothing about me would ever attract attention or bring me admiration. I was told that I would never have the beaux that the rest of the girls in the family had had because I was a ugly duckling. . . . I was ashamed because I had to wear made-over dresses from clothes that my aunts had worn . . . ashamed because I couldn't dance and skate perfectly as others did . . . ashamed because I was different from other girls, ashamed because I was a wallflower. I still remember how thankful I was because a certain boy once asked for a dance at one of those Christmas parties. His name was Franklin D. Roosevelt.

"For over 20 years, I was devastated by self-consciousness and fear. My mother and grandmother and my aunts had been famous beauties in New York society, and I was ashamed to be the first girl in our family who was not a belle. My mother would sometimes say to visitors, 'Eleanor is such a funny child: so old-fashioned that we call her "granny." '

"The big thing that eventually gave me courage was helping people who were worse off than myself. For example, in

1910, my husband was a member of the New York State Senate, and he and 18 other assemblymen were waging a war against Tammany Hall. These assemblymen spent much of their time holding conferences in our home in Albany both day and night. So I visited the wives of these men. I was shocked to find that many of them were spending their days and nights in lonely hotel rooms. They knew no one in Albany except their husbands. . . . I found that by trying to cheer them up and by trying to give them courage, I developed my own courage and self-confidence.

"Fear is the most devastating emotion on earth. I fought it till I won."

The cause of so much low self-esteem in our country is based on three wrong principles governing so many children and teens—intelligence, beauty, and money.

Intelligence. Teachers and parents favor the smartest students. All the others feel like failures. People have different abilities. All should be judged by their application and effort. The *C* student who works just as hard as the *A* student should be given an *A*. The so-called curve grading system is wrong. That teacher has predetermined that a certain number will fail. Students having a more difficult time should be tutored, challenging the teacher to exert more effort in helping them master the course. Grades should be based on the ability to master the course, discipline applied in study habits and effort, and the development of a high level of self-esteem that will enable the student to go on to further achievement.

The problem of failing a student is that the *F* may destroy that student's self-esteem and he may not try again.

Never tell a student he is stupid or dumb. Instead, challenge him to do his best.

When faced with a mountain, we will climb over, we will
fly over, we will find a pass through, we will tunnel through,
or we will dig deep and strike gold or diamonds.

Stanley Coopersmith, professor at the University of California-Davis, in his exhaustive study of self-esteem found:

Students with low self-esteem graded 101.53 on the IQ test.

Students with high self-esteem graded 121.18 on the IQ test.

That is a twenty-point difference, resulting from how they felt about themselves.

Beauty. Everyone but the most beautiful girl and the most handsome guy is considered to be ugly. Beauty should be measured from within, not judged by external features.

Ugly means *frightful, offensive to the sight.* You can go for months and never see a truly ugly person. Yet, many children and teens call themselves ugly. Never call another person ugly. We all have differing looks. Never contrast one child with another. Pointing out the different distinctive features means all have beauty and value.

Money. In our society, the kids with the most money are considered superior. This is a false standard. Money is simply one standard of measuring values, and children and teens from homes with money did nothing to earn it. They simply happened to be born into these homes. We must do everything possible to change this social enigma.

Causes of Low Self-Esteem

1. Negative body image. Feeling inferior in contrast with someone else.
2. Criticism tapes. A pattern of acceptance from parents and others that makes the child feel unworthy because of criticism.
3. Critical blow-ups. Negative self-criticism the child gives him or herself.

It's not the amount of time you devote, but what you devote to the time that counts.

4. Chronic comparisons to others. Make each child know he is valued.
5. Demands of perfection. No one is perfect. Perfectionists are driven by feelings of insecurity, so they try to compensate by being perfect.
6. Sense of hopelessness. Negative input from others has destroyed hope.

Typical Negative Statements

I can't remember names.
It's just no use.
Nothing ever goes right for me.
I'm so clumsy.
I'm just not creative.
I can't seem to get organized.
I can never afford the things I want.
No matter what I do, I can't seem to lose weight.
I just don't have the patience for that.
It's another blue Monday.
I get sick just thinking about it.
I'm just no good.
I never know what to say.
I'd like to stop smoking, but I can't seem to quit.
I don't have the energy I used to have.
I never have any money left at the end of the month.
I'll never win anything.
My desk is always a mess.
I feel like I'm over the hill.
Nobody likes me.
It seems like I'm always broke.
Nobody wants to pay me what I'm worth.
I'm just no good at math.
I get so depressed.

"The secret of success in life is for a man to be ready for his opportunity when it comes."
Prime Minister Benjamin Disraeli

Nothing seems to go right for me.
That's impossible.
I always freeze up in front of a group.
I just can't get with it today.
I just can't take it anymore.
I get a cold this time every year.
I'm really at the end of my rope.
I just can't handle this.
I've always been bad with words.
If only I were taller.
If only I had more time.
It's going to be another one of those days.
I just know it won't work.
That's just my luck.
I don't have any talent.
Everything I eat goes right to my waist.
Today just isn't my day.
I already know I won't like it.
I never have enough time.
That really makes me mad.
When will I ever learn.
Sometimes I just hate myself.
I'm too shy.
With my luck, I don't have a chance.
Things just aren't working out right for me.
I'm really out of shape.
Why should I try? It's not going to work.
I've never been any good at that.
The only kind of luck I have is bad luck.
Someone always beats me to it.
I never get a break.
Everything I touch turns to -----
Sometimes I wish I'd never been born.
I lose weight, but then I gain it back again.

---

*The more you borrow from your bank account of positive
thoughts, the more abundantly it grows.*

I just can't seem to get anything done.
I'm just not a salesman.
There's just no way.
I'm nothing without my coffee in the morning.
I'll never get it right.
I hate my job.
I'm just not cut out for that.
You can't trust anyone anymore.
I never seem to get any place on time.
If only I were smarter.
If only I had more money.
If only . . . on and on. . . .

Habits You May Want to Change

Putting things off
Working too hard or not working hard enough
Ignoring problems
Forgetting names or other important things
Making excuses
Overindulging—eating or drinking too much
Saying "yes" when you want to say "no"
Not listening
Interrupting other people when they're talking
Not telling the truth
Being a gossip
Letting your emotions control you
Giving advice that isn't asked for
Talking too much
Not taking care of details
Smoking
Arguing
Oversleeping
Being a complainer
Losing things

What makes a man great is his ability to decide what
is important and to focus attention on it until it is done.

Being sarcastic
Never being on time
Blaming others
Being disorganized
Worrying
Not setting priorities
Wasting time
Spending more money than you earn
Being overly critical of others
Starting something but not finishing it

Self-esteem has two parts: 1) a sense of personal ability, and 2) knowledge of personal value. High self-esteem is self-respect, self-confidence, self-value, self-acceptance, self-love, and self-celebration. High self-esteem assures us of confidence in coping, in facing life, in the ability to meet life's challenges and opportunities, and to feel that life works. Low self-esteem expresses a feeling that I can't cope, I can't face life's problems, and that I am not fit to function as a person. High self-esteem means living in the now. Low self-esteem means living in the pain.

Stanley Coopersmith's extensive survey on self-esteem gives us the following:

When the father had regular work and enjoyed his work—97% of his children had high self-esteem.

When the father was out of work often and away from home often—18% of his children had high self-esteem.

When the mother had regular work and enjoyed her work—66% of her children had high self-esteem.

When the mother had high self-esteem—66% of her children had high self-esteem.

When the mother showed emotional stability—85% of her children had high self-esteem.

---

*The important thing in life is to have a great aim and
to possess the aptitude and perseverance to attain it.*

When the mother was pleased with her husband's role as a parent—94% of the children had high self-esteem.

When there was no conflict between the parents—82% of the children had high self-esteem.

When the children made A's and B's—58% had high self-esteem.

When the mother created happiness in the home—91% of the children had high self-esteem.

When the children's behavior was nondestructive—88% had high self-esteem.

When the children had a lot of illness and accidents—64% had high self-esteem.

When the parents spent a lot of time with children—82% of the children had high self-esteem.

When the mother showed a lot of affection—79% of the children had high self-esteem.

When the mother and the children had good rapport—88% of the children had high self-esteem.

When the children were held to high standards—80% had high self-esteem.

When the children had constancy of rules—88% had high self-esteem.

When the children had firm and fair parental decisions—85% had high self-esteem.

When the parents dreamed of their children's achievements—88% of the children had high self-esteem.

In 1958, I had an hour-long appointment with former president Harry S. Truman, in his library in Independence, Missouri. I asked him, "Mr. President, what can parents do to raise achieving children?" He pointed to the pictures of his two grandfathers on the wall behind his desk and said, "Parents should take their children to Sunday school and church, instill within them the discipline of hard work, loyalty to family, God, and country, and set a great example."

If you have a dream, you have everything. If you have everything and no dream, then everything means nothing.

When Mrs. Truman came into his study, he introduced her and told me, "In 1952, many of my party wanted me to run again, and I would have won. But Beth said to me, 'Harry, I'm tired. Let's go home.' And we did. I owed that to her." Mrs. Truman had never liked politics but tolerated the time in Washington for Harry's sake. When she expressed her desire to go home, Truman knew it was time to honor her request.

Sources of High Self-Esteem

Every child needs
1. Parental approval
   A. For his/her own sense of personhood
   B. For his/her sense of proven ability
   C. For his/her sense of individuality
   D. To set realistic achievement goals
   E. To provide a framework of meaningful values
2. Other good examples and adult role models
3. Sibling and peer approval
4. Educational achievements
5. Skills, mastery in sports, music, hobbies, etc.
6. To learn to feed self good strokes
7. To receive God's love and acceptance
8. Affirming romantic experiences
9. Career expertise and enjoyment
10. Root-value transfer

Positive Mind Power

The only thing we control in this world is our own minds. Practice these mind power statements daily:

I believe it in my mind; I live it in my conduct; I celebrate it with great feelings. I am a unique, never-to-be-repeated miracle of God. I rejoice in the joy of God's love. I know and receive the love of my parents and family. I love myself as a

---

If you meet someone who has no smile, give him one of yours.

conduct of life. I meet my own needs, because I have a personal emotional maintenance program. I always choose to do the things that are important to me. I choose not to argue. I choose not to lose my temper. I choose to love my job. I choose to get up and go to work each day. I choose my reaction to other people.

I have a good mind and I cultivate its growth. I have a healthy body and I treat it right. I love my family and friends and I put energy, loyalty, and effort into these relationships. I have a good memory and can bring forth everything I need from my mind-computer storage bank.

I love people and am a good listener. I give attention to other people and learn from everyone I meet. I know I am becoming what the people I meet and the books/tapes I experience are. I have the courage to believe and to express my beliefs. I have the wisdom to listen and seek to learn from all the people who come into my life.

I take responsibility for my life, my career, and my relationships. I am good at my career and am constantly growing on my job. I give more than I am paid for on my job as a commitment to excellence. I love life and give my best in everything I do. I set goals for every area of my life and work toward their achievement. I invest time with my family as a vital function of life. I enjoy sharing my values, my time, and my efforts in building better family relationships.

I do not worry; I choose to program a positive course of action instead. I choose to control my thinking and my emotions, so I choose not to worry. I choose to think only those thoughts that please me, so I control my thoughts. My feelings are positive, warm, and exciting because my thoughts are clear, positive, and enlightening. I live a calm, controlled, and serene life. I choose to relax and enjoy life. I choose to pace my schedule so as to invest time in quiet solitude. I choose to enjoy great mood music to enhance my

---

You won't get what you want out of life. You get what you expect.

serenity and peace. I choose to avoid all brassy, conflicting, and chaotic sounds.

My thoughts create wholeness within me. They contribute to my peace, because I control what I think. I choose for my mind to only dwell on harmony, balance, peace, and joy. I look for the simple solution in each situation. I am dedicated to a life of unity, wholeness, harmony, peace, and joyful serenity. I am resolved to find the good in any problem.

I choose to help build a world of peace, unity, optimism, and self-celebration. I choose to do those things that are in my best interest. I determine that all my actions will benefit me and others equally. I will not violate, take advantage, or hurt any other person. I regard the personhood of every person as a sacred trust not to be abused. I am committed to the safety of other people from the brutality of evil people.

I look for and expect the best from my every activity. I look for the best and encourage the best in other people. I will not settle for less than the best in myself and in other people. I seek to create the best in me and in others. I attract the best in others because I live for the best for myself. I draw other people to myself by the power of my love and acceptance of them.

I focus the attention of my mind on those things I can change. I leave alone those things I can't change, and I seek wisdom to know the difference. If there is something I have no control nor influence over, I choose not to fret over it. If there is something I can change to the good of all, I will set about to do it.

I keep my mind so busy thinking positive thoughts that I have no time nor place for negative thoughts. I have learned to dominate my negative thoughts by replacing them with their opposite, positive thoughts. In time, the number of my positive thoughts will be greater than the number of negative

---

"If we all did the things we are capable of doing,
we would literally astound ourselves."

Thomas A. Edison

thoughts and I then will be a positive person. I keep so busy with my positive conduct, I don't have time or energy for negative thinking. Since no thought can dwell in my mind without my consent, I choose to think only positive thoughts.

I really am very special. I like who I am and approve of myself. Every day in every way, I am getting better and better. I am growing every day, because I like myself today and will like myself even more when I celebrate my improved greatness. There is no one like me in all the world; I am special. There will never be another person just like me. I've always wanted to be someone important, and I've given myself approval to do just that. I like how I feel when I achieve my best and I want to feel great all my life. I have many beautiful qualities still within me, breaking out into fulfillment. God has given me many talents and I want to develop them all. As I grow, I am sure I will discover even more talents I have not known to date.

Because I am positive, I radiate good feelings toward everyone I come into contact with. My confidence shows itself as I glow with excitement. I am full of life and I enjoy life every day. I am glad to be alive, because life is a constant growth experience. I am intelligent and I seek the solution to any problem that comes my way. I think good thoughts, do good things, and receive good feelings. I have unlimited energy and enthusiasm to put into my life. I share my excitement for life with everyone I know. I love to be around positive people, because I draw additional strength from them. I even enjoy being around negative people, for my positive energy is shared with them and I have an unlimited source.

I am a warm, sincere, loving person, whose life is unfolding daily like a rosebud. I like to see the growth in other people I share my zest for living with. I love myself as God's intent for my happiness. I love other people as God's command for my conduct. I love life for the joys I experience daily.

Just remember that what you are going to be tomorrow,
you are becoming today.

Conclusion

Now that we know how we got this way—let's do something about it.

Make a commitment to yourself to value yourself and to celebrate yourself. Never put yourself down. Don't say critical things about yourself. You don't deserve it; it's self-destructive and will hinder you from celebrating yourself. The only way you can overcome self-critical statements is to write out the self-critical statements you have been giving yourself. Opposite each of them, write out the opposite, positive statement. Remember, the only way we overcome a negative thought is to replace it with its opposite, positive affirmation. For example, replace "You dummy, you're always making mistakes," with "That's the first mistake I've made in the last fifteen minutes. That's OK, I'm human. I'll make a conscious effort not to make that mistake again. I'm learning."

Keep this list with you at all times. Each time you catch yourself putting yourself down, quote the opposite, positive affirmation. It will take time, but you're on your way.

Choose a program of action that will dethrone the critic in your life. Here are some statements that dethrone the critic:

1. You're kicking me right now to force me to live by the rules I grew up with.
2. You're comparing me to everyone so that once in a while I'll find someone lower on the totem pole than me.
3. You're slapping me around like my parents used to do, and I believe you because I believed them.
4. You're beating me so that I'll achieve more and more and maybe feel better about myself.
5. You're insisting that I be perfect, because if I did everything exactly right, I might finally feel OK about myself.

Every man is the maker of his own fortune.

6. You're saying I can't do it so that I won't bother trying and won't have to worry about screwing up.
7. You're telling me they won't like me so that I won't be so hurt if I'm rejected.
8. You're saying she's disgusted by me so that no matter what the truth is, I'll be prepared for the worst.
9. You're telling me to be perfect so that I'll naively think that maybe I could be perfect and for a few minutes feel better about myself.
10. You're kicking me around so that I can atone for divorcing -----.

You are seeking a life of fulfillment. The inner peace, genuine self-esteem, unlimited achievement, and great human relations all can be yours. That's what we all want. Now take it.

"Problems are only opportunities in work clothes."
Henry J. Kaiser

CHAPTER 3

Giving Yourself Permission to Be Whole

Why You Deserve High Self-Esteem

1. You are a miracle of God. He didn't intend for you to be a fear-filled neurotic, compromising person. In the Bible, the apostle Timothy says in his second epistle, "For God hath not given us the spirit of fear; but of power, and of love, and of a sound mind." (2 Tim. 1:7)
2. You are of value because you exist.
3. You have abilities—many of them untapped—lying dormant, but nevertheless available.
4. With every achievement, you prove your abilities. Make an inventory of all your accomplishments and delight in them.
5. Your only limitations are in your own mind. Set your goals, work your plan, make your commitment, and you will prove your worth.

Your Personal Bill of Rights

1. You have the right to be treated with respect.
2. You have the right not to take responsibility for anyone else's problems or bad behavior.
3. You have the right to get angry.
4. You have the right to say no.
5. You have the right to make mistakes.

6. You have the right to have your own feelings, opinions, and convictions.
7. You have the right to change your mind or to decide on a different course of action.
8. You have the right to negotiate for change.
9. You have the right to ask for emotional support or help.
10. You have the right to protest unfair treatment or criticism.

David Quam was born on a farm in North Dakota. A railroad line ran between his father's farm and adjoining farms. Many afternoons when David was either eight or ten years old, he led other farm boys to play a dangerous game. They would run in front of the five o'clock train. The boy who ran closest to the train was considered the hero and the boy who ran the farthest from the train was considered the coward. Usually, David won, but one afternoon he fell in front of the train and his right arm was severed at the shoulder.

David's parents never let him feel he was disabled. He could tie his shoestrings, milk a cow, saddle his horse, and do anything anyone else could do. In high school, he was all-state guard on the state championship football team. He was all-state forward on his basketball team. He played outfield on the baseball team—à la Pete Gray. Pete Gray played outfield for two years, 1944-1946, for the St. Louis Browns and had a batting average of .229. Pete had a stub of an arm. He would catch the ball in his glove, put the glove in the stub, and pull the ball out and throw in one motion.

David would catch the ball in the webbing, flip the glove, pull the ball out, and throw in one motion.

After high school, David moved to Minneapolis and started in the insurance business. He stayed at the YMCA. One night, about eleven o'clock, he was batting the ball off

Take a hard look at what you truly expect to get out of life, because that's what you'll get.

the walls in the handball court. The athletic director came by and said to David, "You can't play this game with one arm."

David went up to his room and cried himself to sleep. Were his feelings hurt? No, he was angry that someone told him he couldn't play handball.

Within two years David was Y champion. He moved a few blocks down the street and joined the Minneapolis Athletic Club, tougher competition. Within two years he was city champion and went on to become national champion and internationally rated. He was one of the first twelve inductees in the Handball Hall of Fame.

In 1945 Pres. Harry S. Truman called David to Washington and asked him to be a $1-a-year man and go into the veterans' hospitals and tell the guys who had lost arms and/or legs about his story.

David would take his two huge scrapbooks into a room and say, "I'm David Quam. When I was ten, I lost an arm I didn't need anyway, for I can do with one arm what anyone else can do with two." After questioning him, the veterans would say, "Get me up out of this bed and down to therapy."

For two years, he travelled all over the country to tell his story. He then returned to Minneapolis. My friend, Boo Buie, had recently returned to the city from Hawaii. He challenged David to a handball game. At the University of Minnesota, he had been National AAU Handball Champion. Now, his game was the best it had ever been.

David beat Boo 21–7. Over a cup of coffee afterward, Boo said, "David, I thought I could give you a good game. You swamped me." David replied, "Well, I had an advantage over you." Boo responded, "Advantage! You are 69 years of age, with one arm. I'm 38, at the best of my game, with two arms. What's the advantage?"

"It is not how much we have, but how much we enjoy that makes happiness."

Charles H. Spurgeon

With a bit of a grin, David said, "When the ball came to you, you had to decide which hand to use. I didn't have to decide."

David Quam was a master of high self-esteem.

My friend, Bill Glass, played twelve of his thirteen years in the National Football League with the Cleveland Browns, nine of those years with the great Jim Brown, possibly the greatest running back in the history of the game.

Bill told me, "Seventy-two hours before every game, Jim shut out everybody and everything as he ran through his mind all the plays in the playbook, programming his mind for the players on the opposing team. Each of the 250 plays Jim played in his subconscious mind eleven times, each time for each of the opposing players. On an off-tackle slant, he anticipated how the outside linebacker would react and Jim programmed how he would respond. He did this for each player. He had a fraction-of-a-second advantage over his opponent. Rather than react, he anticipated. His mental power was as great or greater than his immense physical abilities."

Jim Brown's supreme self-confidence mentally and physically made him one of the greatest athletes of all time.

How to Improve Your Self-Esteem

1. Change is possible. Take control, decide, and act now.
2. Change takes time. Plan your work and work your plan.
3. Firmly give up low self-esteem. You can choose high self-esteem.
4. Take negative energy generated by low self-esteem and apply it with intensity to building high self-esteem.
5. You are not alone. Get involved in a caring network and help others build their high self-esteem.
6. Have compassion on yourself. You are loved, we are loved, they are loved.

Attitudes are habits of thinking. Remember:
First you form your habits, then they form you.

7. Make a commitment. Do everything you do with the best of your ability.

Self-Facing	**vs.**	**Self-Blaming**
1. Admits undeveloped areas		1. Blames self for failure
2. Admits mistakes		2. Condemns own mistakes
3. Resolves to overcome		3. Quits in misery
4. Realizes need of friendships		4. Rejects friendships
5. Faces unkind actions with others		5. Won't face hostility
6. Commitment to achieve at work		6. Goofs off at work
7. Seeks goals to master time		7. Lets others control time
8. Has long-range plans for success		8. Has no plans for the future
9. Is at peace within		9. Has no peace, only blame

Keys to High Self-Esteem

1. The secret to inner peace lies in self-affirmation. A quiet celebration.
2. You can't change others, but you can change your reaction to others.
3. The path to inner peace requires awareness, courage, decision, and action.
4. Form a positive personal belief system that values and celebrates yourself.
5. In your internal cast of characters, the troublemakers will be your "not OK" and "critical parent" tapes. They are hooked into the love of power. They try to manipulate, control, and win. Your nurturing adult and natural child

---

*"The child wants simple things. It wants to be listened to.
It wants to be loved. It may not even know the words,
but it wants its rights protected and its self-respect
unviolated. It needs you to be there."*

Ron Kuptz

are concerned with the power of love. They are the ones that work for the best interest of you and others.

6. To increase your self-worth, you do not need to change yourself. You need to change your "self-talk" and your negative beliefs about yourself. You can choose to become your own nurturing parent.

7. Change the words "should," "ought," "must," and "have to," to those of the nurturing parent—"wish," "prefer," "want," "choose," "feel," and "desire."

8. You can choose not to react to the judgments of others. You do this by giving space to blame, but refusing to take their bait.

9. Reasonable expectations are nurturing. Unreasonable ones cause pain.

10. When you are upset, check what expectations have gone unmet.

11. Your inner criticizer will ask for perfection in feelings, thoughts, and deeds. Give yourself permission to be less than perfect. Do not cling to past mistakes, but rather release them.

12. Give up the belief that things should always go as you want them to; that others should match your feelings, attitudes, and values; that life and others will always be fair; that others should know how you feel or what you want without being told.

13. Take time for meaningful leisure. Put balance into your life by doing those things that give you release from the pressures of daily work.

14. Improve your family, business, and friend relationships. We draw strength from the positive people around us. Release negative relationships that are destructive to your own feelings.

15. Write out goals for your life: career, family, personal,

Time is your most valuable personal resource.
Use it wisely because it can't be replaced.

and professional goals. If you fail to plan, you are planning to fail.

16. With subliminal videocassettes and audiotapes, condition yourself to positive self-talk. You alone are responsible for your feelings. Impact yourself with affirmations that give you the feelings and assurances of success.

Positive Statements

It takes both rain and sunshine to make a rainbow. A positive person understands that a little disappointment doesn't mean that it won't be a great day. Turn the "rain" into something beautiful. A positive person knows that if there weren't a challenge—there wouldn't be a champion.

If you feel down, keep a smile on your face and lift someone else's spirit. When they feel better, it reflects back to you. British Prime Minister Benjamin Disraeli said, "The secret of success is constancy of purpose." Everyone needs a direction in life, some goal he or she is pursuing. Set some good goals, make some plans, and then pursue them with all your might.

Ralph Waldo Emerson said, "Though we travel the world over to find the beautiful, we must carry it with us or we find it not." Real beauty lies within everyone.

Learn from each mistake. Each time you get a wrong answer, you know one answer that can be eliminated. Remember Edison and the light bulb.

A positive person is a good listener. Listening is a very important part of communication. Be willing to lend a listening ear to others, and in return, they lend a listening ear to you.

A positive person realizes that education alone does not guarantee success: only the application of education can do that.

"There is no security on earth. There is only opportunity."
Gen. Douglas MacArthur

Celebrate the uniqueness of yourself. Remember you are unique—there is no one else in the world like you, and there never will be another exactly like you. Be proud of yourself and your unique personality.

There is a saying, "It is better to light one candle than to curse the darkness." A positive person doesn't complain about unfavorable conditions or circumstances, but rather attempts to improve those conditions through positive actions.

Do not lower your goals to the level of your present abilities, but rather raise your abilities to the height of your goals.

If you make one person smile each day for forty years, you will have made 14,610 people happy.

"The best way to know life is to love many things." (Vincent Van Gogh)

Teachers devote their lives to helping young people acquire the knowledge and skills necessary to be successful in life. Teachers are very special people. Give your teachers a hug or a big "thank you" today.

If you are not perfect and you admit it, that's a perfect thing to say.

Remember that you are swapping a day of your life for what you do today. A day that cannot be replaced. Make it a good swap by having a positive and productive day.

Positive people say, "I can, I will, I'll try." Set a goal and then set out to accomplish it. And positive people make an effort to use positive words and phraseology in their daily language. Talk like a positive person and you will become a positive person. If you behave well and do not break rules, then other people will follow suit. Good behavior is a characteristic of a positive person.

"This is the day which the Lord hath made.
We will rejoice and be glad in it."

Ps. 118:24

"Habit is either the best of servants or the worst of masters," states Nathaniel Emmons. Develop positive, good habits and they will carry you far.

Some people worry so much about rainy days that they fail to enjoy the sunshine of today. Today is a special day—enjoy it.

"Let your hopes, not your hurts, set your goals." (Anonymous)

Smile today for someone in need—for tomorrow you may be the one in need.

Don't skip the first day of the rest of your life. Do your best.

A positive person knows that a healthy mind and body are priceless. Regular exercise and proper nutrition are the keys to keeping fit. Drugs will destroy your mind and body—the only mind and body you have. Be smart and say, "Nope to Dope."

Every action has a reaction. We cannot always control the actions in our lives; but we can control our reactions. Plan to react to all situations with a positive, optimistic attitude.

A positive person realizes that opportunities are available today, and every day. Have the courage and the confidence to seize the "opportunities of the day."

George Bernard Shaw said, "People are always blaming their circumstances for what they are. I don't believe in circumstances . . . look for the circumstances you want, and if you can't find them, make them."

Looking for the bad in life is easy because it's always there. Looking for the good in life is more challenging, because sometimes you have to dig deeper—but the good is there.

Chuck Norris, the karate expert and movie star, says, "Ability is not the major prerequisite in achieving any goal—determination and persistence will over come any obstacle."

"Two men look out through the same bars.
One sees the mud, and one the stars."
Frederick Langbridger

A positive person knows that the best of intentions are no good unless they are acted upon. To think nice thoughts and good deeds is OK, but to act out these thoughts and deeds is great. Arthur Schopenhauer noted, "We seldom think of what we have, but always of what we lack." Don't overlook the abundant blessings of which we all have many.

I have learned that success is to be measured not so much by the position that one has reached in life, as by the obstacles which he has overcome while trying to succeed.

Habits can be your best friend or your worst enemy. Develop good habits: the habits of success. And remember, bad habits can be replaced, it just takes desire, time, and persistence.

Summary

Psychologist Abraham Maslow says that every human needs:

1. A feeling of protection and safety learned in childhood and felt today
2. A sense of belonging to family, God, group, and to self
3. A feeling of love, affection, and acceptance from God, family, friends, and others
4. Respect, feeling of personal value, and self-esteem

People in whom all of these needs are met are self-actualizers and enjoy peak performances.

"Ask, and it shall be given you. Seek, and ye shall find.
Knock, and it shall be opened unto you."

Matt. 7:7

CHAPTER 4

Taking Charge of Your Mind

Have you noticed that at the circus you may see a huge elephant with a small rope tied to his leg and to a small stake in the ground? He could pull that stake out with minimal effort. But he doesn't.

In training the elephant, they attach one end of a chain to his foreleg and the other end to a large tree. The elephant pulls time and again, but to no avail. Finally, the elephant quits pulling, surrendering to the rope rather than experience the pain. He has been mind-conditioned to the rope.

So have many people been mind-conditioned to failure. "The only thing in this world you may totally control is your own mind."

You must relearn that the mind is unlimited. If you don't believe that, then you must learn how to take charge of your mind.

Self-esteem is the reputation we have with ourselves.

Living in the Now	vs.	**Living in the Pain**
1. Thinking it out completely		1. Rejecting reasonable answers
2. Alert to every situation		2. Failing to be aware
3. Respecting others' opinions		3. Not willing to talk
4. Seeking truthful answers		4. Failing to seek truth
5. Clearly looking at all viewpoints		5. Muddled thinking

6. Willing to take responsible risks

6. Making no decision

7. Being honest and open

7. Not willing to face facts

8. Independently acting on facts

8. Depending on others only

9. Accepting responsibility

9. Blaming others

10. Confronting self with facts

10. Rejecting self with blame

11. Eager to correct mistakes

11. Unwilling to see or avoid mistakes

12. Reasoning everything out

12. Acting without reason

In an earlier chapter, I told you the story of David Quam. Boo Buie later moved to San Francisco, where he is the Dale Carnegie sponsor. At a downtown civic club, Boo told the David Quam story. Afterward, a tall, middle-aged man came up to Boo and said, "I'd like to tell you my story. When I was 19, my parents sneaked me out of Germany and sent me to Rotterdam to catch a boat for America. We are Jewish. Within six months after my leaving, my parents, brother and sister, and other relatives were taken by Hitler's SS troops to concentration camps. None of them survived.

"I arrived in New York and took a train to San Francisco, where my uncle was a real-estate broker. The first day here, I went with my uncle to his office. I observed agents calling people with German and French names. When they didn't get an appointment, they threw the slips in the wastebasket.

At the end of the day, I told my uncle, 'I want to start selling real estate tomorrow.' He said, 'You can't speak a word of English. I have enrolled you in a night course to learn English. A year from now, when you have mastered the language, I will train you in real estate. Meantime, I have you a job at a German restaurant as a busboy. Let's go home.' I said, 'You go on. I'll come home later.'

"When everyone had left the office, I picked up from the

Self-love comes from God's love.

wastebaskets the names of the people with German and French names. I could talk to them, because I spoke both languages. When they could not speak either language, I hung up. I got three appointments for the next day from these names.

"Then I took the telephone directory and started calling people with German and French names. By nine o'clock, I had seven appointments for the next day. The first month I sold thirty-three houses and led the state of California in real-estate sales. Still couldn't speak a sentence in English."

Dr. John T. Gates was pastor of the Riverside Church—John D. Rockefeller's church—in New York City many years ago. Dr. Gates suffered a heart attack at age fifty-two and had to retire. Mr. Rockefeller hired Dr. Gates as chaplain for his several companies.

One day, shortly after Dr. Gates joined the companies, Mr. Rockefeller came into his office and asked, "Dr. Gates, what are your plans for retirement?" Remember, this was before the days of social security and pension plans.

Dr. Gates replied, "I have $6,000 in savings and what I will be able to save during these next 13 years."

Mr. Rockefeller asked, "How would you like for me to take your $6,000 and invest it for you?" "Please do, Mr. Rockefeller, I consider you to be the greatest financial mind in the world." "All right, Dr. Gates, and I will give you a verbal annual report as to how well your investment is doing."

Annually, Mr. Rockefeller told Dr. Gates, "Your investment is doing well." Never anything about the amount.

When Dr. Gates came to retirement, the companies gave him a retirement banquet at the Waldorf-Astoria Hotel.

"The person who says it can't be done is liable to be interrupted by someone doing it."

Anonymous

There were the usual expressions of appreciation from a number of people, the watch, and a few other gifts.

Then Mr. Rockefeller came to the podium. He expressed his deep appreciation to Dr. Gates, then pulled from his pocket an envelope and said, "Thirteen years ago, Dr. Gates entrusted his life savings to me to invest for him. Here, Dr. Gates, is the return of your investment." Nothing was said about the amount invested nor the amount earned.

After the people had left, Mrs. Gates couldn't wait to find out how much the check was for. When Dr. Gates opened the envelope, he was dumbfounded. His $6,000 investment in thirteen years had grown to more than $6,000,000.

By taking control of your mind positively, there is no limitation on what you may achieve. Dr. Denis Waitley has stated this so well in the poem, "How to Be a Total Winner," on page 199 of his 1988 book, *Seeds of Greatness: The Ten Best Kept Secrets of Total Success*, published in New York by Picket.

The Chinese bamboo is the fastest-growing plant in the world. Yet, when you plant the seed, it takes five years before the stalk breaks the ground. But watch out. It grows at a rate of thirty-six inches each day, to a total height of 100 feet in just three months.

When you have taken positive control of your mind and have adjusted your conduct activity accordingly, you will win with high self-esteem. Here are the activities necessary for your success:

Goals. Nothing becomes dynamic until it first becomes specific. You must write out your goals, change your conduct activity to reach them, and you will. Personal growth goals, family goals, spiritual goals, career goals, financial goals, etc.

You are no bigger than what it takes to upset you.

As a nineteen-year-old, this young man moved from Wisconsin to Hollywood to pursue his career in show business as a pianist. He spent his last $100 on a piano to practice. He tuned and finished it himself. He went to the five-and-ten store and bought glitter that he sewed to his only blue serge suit until he looked like a rhinestone cowboy.

He went out to the Hollywood Bowl and asked the manager if he could come out some morning when the janitors were cleaning the huge bowl and practice a concert. The manager said, "I don't mind, but you can't use our piano." The young man said, "Thanks, I'll bring my own piano."

One morning, about half past ten, the manager's secretary came into his office and said, "Boss, you've got to hear this." The manager went out to the bowl, listened ten minutes and said to his secretary, "Close the office and invite all the people to come out and hear this. It's too good to miss." He turned to the janitors and said, "Sit down and enjoy the show, we'll pay you for your time."

After another two hours of beautiful music, anecdotes, and jokes, the thirty-five employees gave the young man a standing ovation. He thanked them and said, "I wanted to get the feel of how it will be when I pack this bowl with 17,500 people at $20 a head, and I'll do it within two years." He did and went on to earn more than $75,000,000 as he became the world's best-known pianist. His name was Liberace. He set his goal, put himself in the act of doing it, and did.

Audiotapes. By continually bombarding your mind with positive learning with audiotapes, you can salvage otherwise wasted time. For example, if you drive 10,000 miles a year, you have 400 hours of learning opportunity in your auto; 20,000 miles a year, 800 hours; 30,000 miles a year, 1,200

"The right man is the one who seizes the moment."

Goethe

hours; 40,000 miles a year, 1,600 hours. Four hundred hours is equal to one year's college education. So, you can get the same as a four-year college education each year that you drive 40,000 miles and listen to audiotapes. Convert this time for your success.

Subliminal tapes. Subliminal means *under the line.* The message is recorded and then masked with music and/or ocean waves, which makes learning so much fun. The message flows past the negative thoughts in your conscious mind, directly into the creative power of your subconscious mind.

Videocassette Tapes. When asked by an American research team why World War II ended earlier than expected, General von Rundstead, Chief of the German High Command, answered, "America's use of the 35-mm motion pictures." The Americans were amazed and asked, "What do you mean?" General von Rundstead replied, "We used motion pictures to train our military and industry [demonstrating the power of propaganda]." Germany had anticipated that it would take the United States at least five years to convert to a wartime economy. But the United States was able to accomplish this feat within two years. Rundstead said, "That's how you won the war."

Invest at least thirty minutes a day watching motivational, inspirational videocassette tapes to take charge of your mind.

Concert Learning. Some twenty-two years ago, in Sofia, Bulgaria, Dr. Georgi Lozonov took sixty professional and semiprofessionals and taught them French in one day. He spoke a Bulgarian word and another person stated the French word. None of these sixty people knew any French when they started. At the end of the day, having

"When you are through changing, you're through."
Bruce Barton

repeated 1,000 words, three times each, the group was tested. On average, they each learned 920 French words. Using this system, an entire new language can be learned in a week.

This concept, plus subliminal tape use, is primarily how the East Germans, a country of 16,000,000, have soundly beaten us in the last several Olympiads.

Here's how it works. Play largo music, symphonic recordings at about sixty beats a minute in a stereophonic sound system, and lower the volume so that the words can be heard over the music. What it does is remove the negative thoughts and limiting conditioning and creates a mesmerizing effect for learning.

You can do the same thing in your home. Set the music and play an audiotape with the message you want to learn. The mind you save may be your own.

Behavior That Expresses Self-Esteem

1. Your face, manner, way of talking, and moving project joy in being alive and a simple delight in the fact of being.
2. You are able to speak of accomplishments or shortcomings with directness and honesty.
3. You are comfortable in giving and receiving compliments, expressions of affection, appreciation, and the like.
4. You are open to criticism and comfortable about admitting mistakes.
5. Your words and movements have a quality of ease and spontaneity.
6. There is harmony between what you say and do, how you look, how you sound, and how you move.
7. You exhibit an attitude of openness to and curiosity

"Take time to deliberate: but when the time for action comes, go for it."
Pres. Andrew Jackson

about new ideas, new experiences, and new possibilities of life.

8. You are able to see and enjoy the numerous aspects of life, in self and in others.
9. You project an attitude of flexibility in responding to situations and challenges, a spirit of inventiveness, and even playfulness.
10. You are comfortable with assertive behavior.
11. You express a quality of harmony and dignity under conditions of stress.

Physical Signs of Genuine Self-Esteem

1. If you have alert, bright, and lively eyes.
2. If you have a relaxed face with natural color and good skin vibrancy.
3. If you hold your chin naturally in alignment with your body.
4. If your jaw is relaxed.
5. If you hold your shoulders relaxed, but erect.
6. If you keep your hands relaxed, graceful, and quiet.
7. If your arms hang in a relaxed, natural way.
8. If you maintain posture that is relaxed, erect, and well-balanced.
9. If you walk purposefully (without being aggressive or overbearing).
10. If you keep your voice modulated and maintain an intensity appropriate to the situation.

If these ten signs apply to you, then you have genuine self-esteem. This above list, which has been adapted from its original form, can be found on pages 17-18 of Nathaniel Branden's *Honoring the Self: Personal Integrity and the Heroic Potentials of Human Nature*, published in Los Angeles by J. P. Tarcher in 1984.

In his famous talk, "Acres of Diamonds," Dr. Russell Con-

If you look for the positive things in life, you'll find them.

well tells of a Persian farmer, who had for his guest one
night a holy man. During the evening, the holy man noticed
a piece of glassy rock on the farmer's mantle. He told him
about diamonds and how they were formed and of their
value. The farmer determined he would search the world
over for diamonds. He sold his farm, turned his family over
to relatives, and set out on his worldwide search. Many years
later, having exhausted his search and now out of money, he
walked into the ocean and drowned himself.

Within a few days of his death, the farmer who had
bought his farm unearthed on that very farm a diamond
mine. The glassy rock on the mantle was from that very
field. That diamond mine was Golgonda, one of the richest
diamond mines in the world. The searching farmer could
have met his fondest dreams in his own backyard.

Your diamond mine is between your ears. By taking
charge of your mind, you can achieve your greatest dream.

Positive Statements

Positive people know they will face disappointments, and
that it will depend on the attitude with which one faces a disappointment that will determine whether you overcome the
disappointment or whether it overcomes you.

Alexandre Dumas said, "A person who doubts himself is
like a man who would enlist in the ranks of his enemies and
bear arms against himself. He makes his failure certain by
himself being the first person to be convinced of it."

When a road is being built, construction crews overcome
obstacles such as mountains or rivers by building bridges or
tunnels. Don't let obstacles stop you—find a way to overcome them.

---

*"And in every work that he began in the service of the
house of God, and in the law, and in the commandments,
to see his God, He did it with all his heart, and prospered."*
2 Chron. 31:21

A positive person knows that you can't get anywhere today if you are dwelling on the disappointments and misfortunes of yesterday. Every day is a golden opportunity to start anew and to achieve great things.

No one ever painted a masterpiece the first time he picked up a paintbrush. But, with practice and perseverance, masterpieces have been painted. It is the same with our daily lives. If you stick with your goals, you will achieve them.

On a football field, everyone knows the team's goal—to reach the goal line. The name goal line says it all. In life, everyone needs clear goals as well. Establish goals and put them in writing.

If you really want to be positive, you can be; just think positively, no matter what everyone else around you thinks. If you are positive, it will encourage others to be so, too. Before you know it, you'll have a positive attitude around you.

Enthusiasm is like fuel that keeps the fires of ambition burning. Without enthusiasm, the fire dies out. Get excited and enthusiastic about what you are doing and you will have all the necessary energy to carry you through.

Your attitude is a determining factor in the height of your day's success. Keep your attitude up and you're sure to have an "up" day.

Positive people believe that how you feel on the inside is reflected on the outside by how you dress. So always try to look your best.

Positive people believe it is more important to know where you are going than to see how fast you can get there.

Some people may have the grades and popularity, but they are not the best unless they have a positive attitude. Those with a positive attitude are the real winners.

A positive person knows that he is rich because of who and what he is; not what he has.

"Defeat never comes to any man until he admits it."
Joseph Daniels

Positive people know that the single most important cause of a person's success or failure has to do with the question of what he believes about himself. Believe in yourself.

There is a difference between loving oneself and being in love with oneself. The first example is called a healthy self-esteem; the second example is called self-centered.

It doesn't cost anything to think positively, but the cost of thinking negatively will surely bankrupt you of success.

Instead of spending time fixing blame when something is wrong, one should spend his time trying to fix what is wrong.

A positive person doesn't waste the sunshine of today by worrying about the rainy days that may come tomorrow.

Knute Rockne said, "When the going gets tough, the tough get going." When you are faced with a problem or adversity, don't despair or give up. Instead, be resolved to give it your best effort.

Live the best way you can—positively.

Throughout our lives, we are faced with a series of great opportunities brilliantly disguised as impossible situations. Remember, nothing is impossible to one who believes (Mark 9:23).

For most people, being negative is easy. These are the people who take the easy way out. Being positive takes work, and it's a challenge. Don't be lazy—accept the challenge.

"The best and most beautiful things in the world cannot be seen or even touched. They must be felt with the heart." (Helen Keller)

The secret of success is having goals and believing that you will achieve them. Anything the mind can conceive—if you believe, you will achieve.

Lee Burgland said, "Obstacles are the things we see when we lose sight of our goals." A positive person focuses on the

---

There is no limit to what you can do if you don't
care who gets the credit.

goals he wants to achieve—not the obstacles that he may encounter on the way.

A happy person is not a person who is without any problems. A happy person is one who deals with problems in a positive manner: expecting the best out of all situations.

Wake up, look in the mirror, and say, "I like me," and your day will go great.

A positive person knows that when you always speak the truth, you never have to be concerned with your memory.

Helen Keller was one who did not allow her disabilities to control her life. Instead, she concentrated on her abilities and she became one of the greatest inspirations of all time. Make the most of what you have.

Just as the old wagon trails heading west became rutted to the point that they were unusable: by traveling the same path each day of your life, you too will find yourself stuck in a "rut." Take chances, explore new opportunities, and try something new today.

Learn to build bridges instead of walls. Believe the best, ignore the rest, and you've passed the test to find life's zest.

I am a positive person, as positive as can be. You can be one, too. Just follow me.

Your attitude now will reflect upon you later in life. So, if you want to look forward to a great life, start now by having a positive attitude.

Conclusion

Your subconscious mind is a vast reservoir of all your thoughts and experiences. We are the totality of what we have been through. Blot out of your mind those unpleasant experiences with the power of forgetfulness and recall all those pleasant experiences.

Take a joy inventory. Begin at the age of your earliest remembrance and write out all the joyful experiences you can

"An invincible determination can accomplish almost anything."
Thomas Fuller

remember. Continue to write for each age of your life. Ponder, recall, and delight in these experiences. Go over them again and again. Bombard your consciousness with these events. You will be amazed with the beautiful feelings that will follow.

Determine that the remaining years of your life will be invested in delightful experiences of joy and happiness. You then will have a life worth living.

"I will let no man control me by making me hate him."
Booker T. Washington

CHAPTER 5

How to Raise Your Children to Have High Self-Esteem

> Isn't it strange that princes and kings, and clowns that caper in sawdust rings, and common people like you and me are builders for eternity?
>
> To each is given a bag of tools, a shapeless mass, and a book of rules; and each must make ere life is flown, a stumbling block or a stepping stone.
>
> R. L. Sharpe

The enabling parents. To *enable* means *to give sanction to.* Many enabling parents are unwittingly aiding their children to fail and have low self-esteem.

First we must define what every child needs. Every child needs to know:

I am loved. Love is not primarily an emotion. Love is a conduct. To love is to act in a manner so that the safety, security, satisfaction, and growth of another person is assured.

Love is a decision. It is a commitment to treat another person in his/her highest and best interest.

Love is unconditional. A child is to be loved because he/she exists. A child is a gift of God and must be treated as such. If you love your child only when he/she obeys, then you have put a condition on love.

You may love a child better when his/her conduct is correct. You certainly like a child when the conduct is correct.

You tell the child of your dislikes. You love a child with no conditions.

Love is forever. There are no time restraints, no limits, and no conditions. It is consistent and constant.

Love is a gift, based on the sense of worth. Because they are, they are loved. The greatest gift you grant your child is love with no strings.

Love affirms, not possesses. Love allows and develops independence.

Love is never having to say you're sorry you abused your child.

Love is never having to say you're sorry you blamed, condemned, and criticized.

Love is never having to say you're sorry you filled your child with guilt.

Love is never having to say you're sorry for destroying your child's imagination and creativity.

Love is never having to say you're sorry for driving your child away from the safety, security, and harmony of the home.

I am capable. This includes being capable to feel, able to meet his/her own needs; capable to feel independent as a person; capable to achieve excellence in grades, work skills, and play conduct; capable of owning good feelings of self-worth, self-value, and self-celebration; capable of warmly responding to parent's affection, hugs, and kisses; capable of having confidence to face life's opportunities and responsibilities.

I am able. A child needs to be able to relate effectively with other people, both children and adults; able to maintain his own inner-directed emotional support system; able to achieve his best in school, hobbies, sports, etc.; able to enjoy the beauties of nature and God's love and forgiveness.

"Nothing in this world is so powerful as an idea whose time has come."
Victor Hugo

Enabling parents do the following:

1. Excuse their children for bad grades by blaming the schools, TV, or other reasons.
2. Allow their children to stubbornly disobey their parents, teachers, and God's guidelines of conduct.
3. Fail to instill within their child self-discipline by not organizing a fair and firm code of conduct.
4. Allow their children to fight with other children, sass adults, and prove unmanageable with no recourse of action.

Parents must take intervention action. In other words, parents need to come in or between in order to stop, settle, or modify.

When the child's conduct is contrary to the laws of God, laws of the country, rules of schools, and rules of the home, a loving parent intervenes. Children want the acceptance and approval of their parents. When they do not get that, they will stoop to destructive behavior to receive attention. Intervening parents stop, control, and redirect that behavior that is not in the child's best interest.

In 1937, Lou Gehrig, the outstanding first baseman of the New York Yankees, was asked to go to the Children's Hospital in Chicago, while there to play the White Sox, and visit a boy with polio. Tim, ten years old, had refused to try therapy to get well. Lou was his hero and Tim's parents hoped that Lou would visit Tim and urge him to try the therapy.

Tim was amazed to meet his hero. Lou told Tim, "I want you to get well. Go to therapy and learn to walk again." Tim said, "Lou, if you will knock a home run for me today, I will learn to walk again." Lou promised.

All the way to the ball park, Lou felt a deep sense of

"To become what we are capable of becoming is the only end of life."
Spinoza

obligation and even apprehension that he would be able to deliver his promise that day. Lou didn't knock a home run that day. He had two.

Two years later, when Lou Gehrig was dying with the dreaded muscular disease that to this day bears his name, on July 4, 1939, they celebrated Lou Gehrig Day at Yankee Stadium. Eighty thousand fans, the governor, the mayor, and many other celebrities paid their respects. Lou was one of America's great heroes.

Just before the mike was turned over to Lou to respond, Tim, by this time twelve years old, walked out of the dugout, dropped his crutches, and with leg braces walked to home plate to hug Lou around the waist.

That's what Lou Gehrig meant when he exclaimed those immortal words: "Today I am the luckiest man on the face of the earth."

Lou Gehrig had intervened with Tim. He claimed and received a conduct favorable for Tim from Tim.

Guidelines for Building
Your Child's Self-Esteem

1. Parents set the standards. Never put the child down. Help him to learn the desired conduct and set the right example.
2. Other siblings must not be allowed to crush the confidence of the child.
3. Discount early social blunders and don't allow them to scar.
4. Magnify values and accomplishments so that money and things will not be out of proportion.
5. Any physical defects, such as bucked teeth, must be corrected or turned into a distinctive advantage.

"Have the daring to accept yourself as a bundle of possibilities and undertake the game of making the most of it."
Henry Emerson Foodick

6. Help your child to develop social skills so embarrassment will not follow.
7. Be constantly sensitive to your child's feelings and give him unconditional love and acceptance.
8. Don't allow time pressure to snuff out the essential time needed each day to give your child undivided personal attention.
9. Don't load your child with guilt and fear.
10. Teach your children the "no knock" attitude. Never allow them to put themselves down.
11. Help your children to compensate. The strongest drive of human nature is to compensate for a feeling of inferiority. Lead them to excel within themseleves, to make up by their own conduct what they may first think of as a disadvantage.
12. Be constantly in touch with your child's teacher and be a partner in his growth and achievement.
13. Develop your child's sense of independence. Encourage your child to stand on his own two feet and to effectively grow away from parental dependence. Help him to take pride in himself and his achievements.

Typical Sources of Low Self-Esteem

Most low self-esteem stems from unfortunate childhood experiences. The greatest gift we, as parents, can give our children is sound self-esteem.

1. A parent's own low self-esteem is a model for the child.
2. A child's lack of recognition and appreciation by parents and others as an intrinsically valuable and important individual can mar his self-esteem. Phrases like "A child should be seen and not heard," "Mother knows best," etc., demonstrate that the child's needs,

---

The people who succeed are those who have the self-discipline to develop themselves.

feelings, desires, and opinions not given due consideration.

3. If a child's parents, family, or friends make adverse comparisons with his peers or a favorite brother or sister—this, combined with child's own self-deprecating comparisons with those of his own age whom he admires for their strength and ability, their popularity, self-confidence, or achievements can overpower the child with a devastating sense of inferiority.

4. A child feels inadequate because he is not encouraged and motivated to be independent, to do what he can for himself—to take responsibility for his own needs and well-being to the greatest extent of his ability as he increases in age and experience. The child is not taught to think for himself.

5. The false concepts, values, and reactions of child's parents, teachers, and peers cause him to identify with his actions. For example, Johnny, whose mother has a severe migraine, is a "bad boy," because he slammed the door. Whereas, in reality, it was only his natural exuberance and lack of awareness that caused the act. This may load the child with self-condemnation, shame, guilt, and remorse.

6. Harsh and demanding parents set unreasonable standards, often raising them before the child has developed the ability to meet them. Parents may also subject their children to unreasonable, harsh criticism and undue and/or inconsistent punishment. Such actions cause early frustration, defeatism, and a destructive sense of inadequacy and inferiority.

7. A child being pushed beyond his capacity by the parents' vicarious need to achieve a sense of worth and importance through the child's achievements often causes

---

"To thine own self be true."

Shakespeare

a deep feeling of inadequacy and unworthiness in the child.

8. Rivalry and unsuccessful emulation of an extremely bright or gifted brother or sister, or of an exceptionally talented and prominent parent often generates a deep sense of hopelessness and inferiority.

9. A child's unflattering physical appearance and/or "odd" apparel, plus perhaps physical, mental, or emotional handicaps damage his sense of self-worth.

10. Child is raised on the basis of "reward and punishment," rather than being motivated through understanding and allowed to make his own mistakes and to accept and resolve, or suffer the consequences.

11. Adverse economic, social, cultural, or ethnic position of parents and family often invite depreciation and ridicule.

12. Overpossessiveness, overpermissiveness, and overcontrol exercised by one, or both parents, nurtures a feeling of unimportance and lack of esteem in the child.

13. A serious sense of guilt is frequently induced by one's material wealth or affluent background.

14. High values placed on money, achievement, and things rather than on the individual and his innate worth, can preclude or destroy one's self-esteem.

15. Repeated defeats and failures can destroy one's sense of self-worth and result in one or two extremes. The child may become a dropout from school or society, or he may become a compulsive overachiever in a desperate attempt to "prove himself."

16. Procrastination and lack of self-discipline, taking the path of least resistance, tend to demolish one's self-respect and sense of worth.

"Do one thing at a time, and do that thing as if your life depended upon it."

Eugene Grace

17. Lack of a sense of meaning and purpose in life, of clear goals and objectives, preclude sound self-esteem.

How to Build Great Self-Esteem in Your Child

1. Be an example of self-value, self-love, and self-celebration.
2. Respect your child as a unique, never-to-be-repeated miracle of God.
3. Lead your child to feel loved, valued, and respected for his/her own self.
4. Make your child responsible for his/her actions and conduct.
5. Help your child to feel capable of accomplishing things on his/her own.
6. Show your child that each day is full of joys and wonderful experiences.
7. Give sincere praise and appreciation for every good experience.
8. Let your child find himself through your guidance. Don't make him a robot or rubber stamp of you.
9. Invest time and energy to help your child achieve greatness.
10. Lead your child to improve with each event, not compete with others who may be more beautiful, smarter, or wealthier. These are false standards of greatness and make one all but feel like a loser. The winner is the one who is doing his best for his own sake.
11. Be consistent in your discipline and lead your child to agree as to proper conduct.
12. Praise for good behavior and don't destroy the value of praise by taking away praise when improper conduct occurs.

"I always try to turn every disaster into an opportunity."
John D. Rockefeller

13. Teach children not to use self put-downs. Teach them how to give themselves self-support, self-value, and self-assurance.

When Don was born, the cord was wrapped twice around his neck. Forty-five minutes later, his face was still blue. The doctor hoped there would be no brain damage.

Don's three sisters progressed much faster than he did in most everything. Studying came easy for them, as well as good grades, while Don had to work so much harder for even *C*'s.

When he was eight, his parents had brain-wave tests made. The report was that he was a borderline learning-disabled child, would not be able to reach college, and probably couldn't finish high school.

His parents took him to Dr. Clyde Naramore's Clinic in Los Angeles where a full week was spent in testing. The result: yes, he did have a learning difficulty, but with parental tutoring, encouragement, praise, and especially travel, he could do college work. "Travel?" his parents asked. "Yes. Travel will open up the world to him and create his desire to discover and learn."

So, when Don was eleven, his parents took him and his older sister Claire to Europe and the Middle East. That boy must have asked a million questions.

He was thrilled when he returned to go into classrooms with his slides and tell of his experiences.

At age thirteen, he was taken back to Europe. At fourteen, he went on a trip around the world with his three sisters. At fourteen, also, he went on a trip with his dad to the Olympics in Mexico City. When he was sixteen, he and his sister Claire backpacked and stayed in hostels in Europe for two months. At seventeen, with his own savings

"You must take responsibility for your own development.
Today a reader, tomorrow a leader."

W. Fusselman

from working afternoons and weekends, he went to Europe, the Middle East, and worked on a kibbutz in Israel for a month. On that trip, he was gone a total of five months in all.

He enrolled in junior college, finished with good grades, went on to Georgia State University and graduated with a B.A. in marketing with a *B* average. He would stay up all night for two or three nights in a row preparing for exams. Then he went on to George Washington University, where he graduated with an *A* average in international marketing.

Today, Don is an executive with an international health organization, headquartered in Bangkok, Thailand. He is helping wipe out diseases in the Third World.

He is happily married and the father of two wonderful children. He has supreme self-esteem. Don is Donald Lamar Douglas, my son.

What did we do to help Don overcome learning difficulties that surely could have wracked him for life with low self-esteem?

1. His parents were always available to tutor, encourage, challenge, and praise his every achievement.
2. Every evening at dinner, we discussed the happy learning experiences at school that day.
3. He was not expected to take part in activities that he felt he was not talented in. For example, he went out for junior high school football, found he didn't excel in it, didn't care for it, and was encouraged to drop out rather than forced to stay in football.
4. Home was made into a happy place, a place where the gang was encouraged to gather and participate. We turned three double-car garages into game rooms, with a

---

"No man can really be big who does not read widely outside his own field."

Theodore N. Vail

pool table, stereo music system, etc. Most nights, the children were at home playing with their friends rather than having to find a place to "hang out."

5. Travel opened up the world and its opportunities.
6. Every achievement was praised and recognized. The children were rewarded with ten dollars when they received an *A*, and with five dollars for a *B*. They owed me five dollars for each *D* and ten dollars for each *F*. I believe we had one *D* in all of their school years. The forty or fifty dollars I invested each reporting time was the finest investment I ever made. All four are college graduates, and three have their master's degrees.

Live by the affirmations for the month. Take one each day, quote it with your children, and seek to live by it. The resulting good feelings your children experience will go a long way toward assuring them high self-esteem.

Affirmations for the Month

1. TODAY, I, ＿＿＿＿＿＿ , was created with an unlimited capacity for love, joy, and fulfillment.
2. TODAY, I, ＿＿＿＿＿＿ , accept the truth of this affirmation and live for growth and wholeness.
3. TODAY, I, ＿＿＿＿＿＿ , release and remove all barriers of fear so I can receive all blessings.
4. TODAY, I, ＿＿＿＿＿＿ , live in the positive truths of love, joy, peace, serenity, and prosperity.
5. TODAY, I, ＿＿＿＿＿＿ , receive and give self-confidence, self-love, and self-celebration.
6. TODAY, I, ＿＿＿＿＿＿ , reward myself for every accomplishment and every achievement.
7. TODAY, I, ＿＿＿＿＿＿ , am learning to love myself more in every way as a gift of God's love.
8. TODAY, I, ＿＿＿＿＿＿ , respect my own uniqueness, individuality, and personhood.

Make your life an unfolding greatness.

9. TODAY, I, _____ , meet my own emotional needs, because I will not be dependent on anyone.

10. TODAY, I, _____ , no longer am dependent on others to affirm me, because I do that myself.

11. TODAY, I, _____ , like, value, and please myself and renounce forever self-criticism.

12. TODAY, I, _____ , have unconditional warm feelings for myself, my friends, and all I meet.

13. TODAY, I, _____ , am 100-percent alive, alert, and excited, because I abound in unlimited enthusiasm.

14. TODAY, I, _____ , am unusual and confident, receiving an increasing amount of abundance.

15. TODAY, I, _____ , have replaced all negative thoughts with their opposite, positive thought.

16. TODAY, I, _____ , maintain control of my actions and emotions to achieve my greatness.

17. TODAY, I, _____ , live a life constantly enlarging as I seek beauty, joy, love, and peace.

18. TODAY, I, _____ , enjoy the beauty of fun, friendships, laughter, pleasure, and radiant joy.

19. TODAY, I, _____ , decide what thoughts will enter my mind and receive those I choose.

20. TODAY, I, _____ , release the true greatness within me as my self-appreciation expands.

21. TODAY, I, _____ , enrich my life as all of my activity and conduct is results-oriented.

22. TODAY, I, _____ , am moving on to a higher level of fulfillment as my life unfolds.

23. TODAY, I, _____ , am energized by newfound purpose, goals, dreams, and dynamic excitement.

24. TODAY, I, _____ , welcome the power of change and will ride the crest of opportunities.

25. TODAY, I, _____ , believe and receive the unlimited prosperity that surrounds me.

Everything is his who desires it.

26. TODAY, I, _____ , excitingly live this day in the beautiful unfolding of God's love.
27. TODAY, I, _____ , bless all mankind with my thoughts, prayers, and encouragement.
28. TODAY, I, _____ , look for, seek out, encourage, and recognize every sign of good in others.
29. TODAY, I, _____ , experience empathy, understanding, compassion, and love for all people.
30. TODAY, I, _____ , delight in the joyous feelings I receive and give to all my friends.
31. TODAY, I, _____ , love everyone unconditionally, as a conduct of my love for myself.

Conclusion

Nathaniel Branden, Virginia Satir, Haim Ginott, and Stanley Coopersmith have found that children who experienced being loved and accepted with assurance are able, capable, and have the formula for high self-esteem.

It's not family wealth, education, where we live, social class, parent's occupation, or always having a mother at home. These are not primary and may be of little value.

The four thought processes that every child needs:

1. I am loved, I am of value, I share strong feelings, I am able, and I am capable.
2. I have accepted clear, definite guidelines of conduct. I have freedom and security, confidence, and high standards.
3. I respect myself, my God, and all other human beings and I find within myself the motivation to do my best and to be myself.

"Progress results from persistence with purpose."
Frank Tyger

4. I received from my parents and other adult role models examples and experiences of genuine high self-esteem.

"Nothing is impossible to a willing heart."
John Heywood

CHAPTER 6

Build High Self-Esteem with Effective Work Production

Sigmund Freud said, "Man's link to reality is found in his work." We spend more time at work than any other thing we do except sleep. If you are unhappy on your job, you will be unhappy in everything else you do. Determine that you will love your job. Either change your attitude (for positive joy) about your job or change your job.

Work Values Questionnaire

Put a "check mark" by those values you personally believe in. Put an X by those you do not endorse. Put an O by those that are unimportant to you.

___ Career success

___ High individualism

___ Winning

___ My family's success

___ Providing well for my children

___ Keeping all commitments

___ Having balance in my life

___ Having a wide range of friends

___ Supervising other people well

___ Intellectual growth

___ Financial security

___ Personal attractiveness

___ Ability to influence others effectively

___ Eagerness to set a leading pace

___ Being a good team player

___ Awareness of my heritage

___ Developing many skills

___ Pride in my work production

___ Ability to get things done

___ Habits of thrift

___ Financial wealth

___ Self-sufficiency

___ Fame in my career

___ Being creative

___ Vital health and energy

___ Becoming an effective leader

___ Strong discipline

___ Projecting the right image

___ Marital harmony

___ Honoring my parents and family

___ Open-mindedness

___ Being loyal to my country

___ Being loyal to my God

___ Keeping good records

___ Orderly home life

___ Accuracy of work

Keys to Success on the Job

Never put yourself down. Never consider failure. You are able.

Take an accurate inventory of all of your strong points: talents, abilities, etc.

Take an accurate inventory of those undeveloped areas of your life. They are not weaknesses, but undeveloped areas. Areas you have not gotten around to develop yet. Improve on them one at a time.

Set your mind on succeeding in your work. Goethe said, "He who has a firm will molds the world to himself." Write out what great success in your work means to you. Spell it out. Make it definite. Nothing becomes dynamic unless it first becomes specific. Imagine yourself at the top of your career by the time you retire. Let nothing in the world keep you from achieving it.

Write out your goals. Long range goals are five years or longer; intermediate goals are from one to five years; and short range goals are monthly, weekly, daily, and even

---

"Do a little more each day than you think you possibly can."
Lowell Thomas

hourly. Ask yourself the question, "Am I doing the most important activity in this hour to reach my goals in life?"

There are many types of goals. Goals in your work could mean better production, greater human relationships, more effective customer service, or increased work production on the part of your associates.

Goals for your family could include better income, better grades for your children, more savings, a new car or home, and vacations.

Goals for your personal life may be to spend more time with your family, spiritual growth, and personal growth. Make goals in every area you would like to improve in.

Claim the fantastic power of the creative mind. When faced with a problem, incubate it in your past experience. Talk it over with others. You will soon come up with the correct answer. There is no problem bigger than you and God combined. Together, you form an unbeatable combination.

Start each day with positive plans and end the day with a positive review of your accomplishments. Live each day in day-tight compartments. Don't rehash worries from yesterday and don't anticipate worries for tomorrow. Remember Jesus's admonition: "Take therefore no thought for the morrow; for the morrow shall take thought for the things of itself. Sufficient unto the day is the evil thereof" (Matt. 6:34).

Every day, say to yourself several times, "This is the day that the Lord has made; I will rejoice and be glad in it" (from Ps. 118:24). Doing this will brighten each day and unleash the creative powers within you. The only limitations we have are those in our own minds. We were made for greatness. Claim yours this day and every day.

Practice and live with expectation and assurance of good things coming your way. Raises and promotions come to those who give more than they are paid for.

"Difficulties mastered are opportunities won."
Prime Minister Winston Churchill

Act enthusiastic and you'll be enthusiastic. Put excitement in everything you do. Benjamin Disraeli said, "Every production of genius must be the production of enthusiasm."

Olin T. Binkley was born and reared on a poor mountain farm in Western North Carolina. His parents, having only a grade school education, dreamed that their children would go to college. Olin learned high self-esteem from the love received in his home and the discipline of hard work that he applied to his studies. He led his class every year in school. Upon graduating from high school, he received a partial scholarship from Wake Forest University. That, with several hundred dollars he had earned working every odd job he could find, was all he had to start college.

He came home for the Christmas holiday the first year with his trunk. He told his parents he was out of money and would not go back to college until he had earned considerably more. His mother urged him to reconsider and made Olin promise not to unpack his trunk yet.

At breakfast on the morning he was to go back to school, he turned over his plate, after grace, and was shocked to discover fifty silver dollars. He looked at his father; he was eating; he knew nothing about the money. He looked at his mother. Tears were flowing down her cheeks, and love flowed from her eyes. The smile on her lips was a tremendous encouragement for him to go back to college.

Then he looked at her folded hands on her down-turned plate. They were stained black. Black from countless hours of staying up many a night, picking fifty dollars of black walnuts.

Olin went back to Wake Forest, took another part-time job and finished at the top of his classes. He went on to graduate school and earned his doctorate. He became a seminary professor and a seminary president. Olin was driven with

---

To know and not to do is really not to know.

high self-esteem by a poor mountain mother who had picked fifty dollars of black walnuts.

I had the privilege of teaching several Dale Carnegie leadership classes for the Fort Lauderdale, Florida, Police Department. The positive changes in these officers was amazing.

At the fifth session, on human relations, we challenged the officers to take one of the human relations rules and practice it with other people.

At the sixth session, reporting on the use of human relations, one officer, who worked the beach patrol, gave the following report:

"I have had no use for the 'hippies' I confront on the beach. I try to run in as many as I can. Then I decided to apply the human relation rule: 'Make the other person feel important.'

"I have been 'running in' this hippie for three years. I decided to try this rule. I asked him, 'Tell me more about yourself.' He said, 'I graduated from New York University of Architecture, was engaged to this lovely woman, and had set the date for our marriage the week after graduation. Then, I received this 'Dear John' letter. I fell apart, dropped out of school three weeks before I was to graduate, got on drugs, and came to Florida to hide.' "

"I replied, 'Man, if I was an architect, I would be building beautiful office buildings, hotels, churches, and homes to make people happy. Then you could look back on these and get real joy from the impact of your life.'

"I knew this impressed him, for he expressed it with a troubled look on his face. Each day this past week, I have

---

"Happiness comes of the capacity to feel deeply, to enjoy simply, to think freely, to risk life, to be needed."
Storm Jammeson

talked with him further, and maybe I'm getting across to him. I know I feel good about this rule."

The fourteenth session was graduation, when each officer told what he had received from the course.

When this beach officer came to give his talk, he said, "Do you folks remember the story I told you at the 6th session, how I changed my attitude about this 'Hippie' and his response?

"Last week, I was working the beach and this good-looking guy, with neat hair, clean-shaven, dressed in a three-piece suit, came up to me and said, 'You remember me?' I replied, 'No, I've never seen you before.' He answered, 'I'm the guy who was trained as an architect that you took a personal interest in. You really shook me up. I decided to get off drugs, went to a clinic, was allowed to take my exams, received my degree. Amazingly, my old girlfriend had not married that guy she dumped me for, and we are back together. And, I have a new job with the finest architecture company in Fort Lauderdale.'

"Last night, my wife and I went to dinner with that couple. They are here tonight and I want you to meet, in person, the results of the rule, 'Make the other person feel important.'" And he had them stand.

Chief of Police Parker, who was there, came up to me afterward and said, "Douglas, the expense of the entire course was worth it in the effect of this one life."

The architect discovered high self-esteem in the challenge of a police officer and the love of his lady.

Some Important Quotes on Work

The destiny of my life is up to me.

Belief in heroics makes heroes.

Vince Lombardi opened each training camp with this sort of speech:

Our only limitations are self-imposed.

Gentlemen, we are going to have a great football team. We are going to win games. Get that. You are going to learn to block. You are going to learn to tackle. You are going to outplay the teams that come against you. Get that. How is this to be done? You are to have confidence in me and enthusiasm for my system. The secret of the whole matter will be what goes on in your head. Hereafter, I want you to think of three things: your home, your religion, and the Green Bay Packers. In that order. Let enthusiasm take hold of you— beginning now.

"A man uses his work to define for himself who he is and what he will do with his life."　　　Dr. Harry Levinson

"Success, in the long run, is a measure of one's ability to turn task into adventure."　　　Dr. John Bjorksten

"The purest pleasure lies within the circle of useful occupation."　　　Henry Ward Beecher

"A man is a worker. If he is not that, then he is nothing."
　　　Joseph Conrad

"An hour's industry will do more to produce cheerfulness than a month's mourning."　　　Barrows

"There is no development without effort and effort means work."　　　Pres. Calvin Coolidge

"All the geniuses I have encouraged have been the hardest workers and most indefatigable students I have known."
　　　Archibald Henderson

"It is the man whose enthusiasm lasts for thirty years that becomes a leader."　　　Edward Burgess Butler

"If we all did the things we are capable of doing, we would literally astound ourselves."　　　Thomas A. Edison

---

"Without enthusiasm, there is no progress in the world."
Pres. Woodrow Wilson

"The world stands aside to let anyone pass who knows where he is going."   David Starr Jordon

"Without enthusiasm, there is no progress in the world."
                                      Pres. Woodrow Wilson

"A man can succeed at almost anything for which he has unlimited enthusiasm."   Charles Schwab

"When a man dies, if he can pass enthusiasm to his children, he has left them an estate of incalculable value."
                                      Thomas A. Edison

"I like a man who bubbles over with enthusiasm. Better be a geyser than a mud puddle."   John G. Sheed

"Every great and commanding moment in the annals of the world is the triumph of some enthusiasm."
                                      Ralph Waldo Emerson

"Face the thing that seems overwhelming and you will be surprised how your fear will melt away."   Dale Carnegie

"No man is worth his salt who is not ready at all times to risk his body, to risk his well-being, to risk his life, in a great cause."   Theodore Roosevelt

"Saints are sinners who believe in God and keep trying."
                                      Anonymous

"The harder I work, and the better I plan, the luckier I get."
                                      Anonymous

"I use all the brains I have, and all I can borrow."
                                      Pres. Woodrow Wilson

"Some people regard discipline as a chore. For me, it is a kind of order that sets me free to fly."   Julie Andrews

---

"A free society is one where it is safe to be unpopular."
                                      Adlai Stevenson

"The greatest happiness comes from the greatest activity."
Bovee

"Life is too short to be little." Benjamin Disraeli

"It is a funny thing about life. If you refuse to accept anything but the best, you will get it." Somerset Maugham

"Happiness is a perfume you cannot pour on others without getting a few drops on yourself." Ralph Waldo Emerson

"For a big job, find a busy man." Anonymous

"No man stands as tall as he who makes other people more productive." Anonymous

"If you work hard enough, and smart enough, success is sure to follow." Anonymous

"Luck is where opportunity, preparation and dedication meet." Anonymous

"The surest way to knock the chip off another fellow's shoulder is by patting him on the back." Anonymous

"Success comes from mastering fundamentals, developing physical and mental toughness, hard work, and making the second effort." Vince Lombardi

"The greatest discovery of my generation is that human beings can alter their lives by altering their attitudes of mind." William James

"The ability to get along with and motivate people is life's greatest ability." Dale Carnegie

"What makes a man great is the ability to decide what is important and to focus attention on it until it is done."
Anonymous

"The important thing in life is to have a great aim and to

"Do the thing you fear, and the death of fear is certain."
Ralph Waldo Emerson

possess the aptitude and perseverance to attain it."

Anonymous

"The person who says it can't be done is liable to be interrupted by someone doing it."   Anonymous

"Every misfortune always carries the seed of an equal or greater benefit."   Napoleon Hill

The only thing we totally control is our mental attitude.

Be a Good Listener

Reasons why listening will pay off for you:

1. To learn something
2. To understand better
3. To be entertained
4. To get information
5. To show respect for the other person
6. To be a team player
7. To ask intelligent questions
8. To discover other people's needs
9. To increase productivity
10. To be more effective
11. To make accurate evaluations
12. To make effective comparisons
13. To understand and be understood
14. To get the best value
15. To enhance relationships
16. To solve problems
17. To show you care and are involved
18. To make intelligent decisions
19. To prevent waste and loss
20. To make more money
21. To avoid being embarrassed
22. To stay out of trouble

"A wise man will make more opportunities than he finds."
Francis Bacon

23. To save time
24. To be a supportive friend
25. To be in "win-win" situations
26. To increase your concentration abilities
27. To build rapport with people
28. To settle disagreements
29. To improve my personality
30. To use the gift of hearing

Do you have a good listening attitude?

A Quiz to Help You Determine Your Listening Attitude

(Answer Yes or No.)

	Y	N
1. I am interested in many subjects and make an effort to not knowingly tune out dry-sounding information.	—	—
2. I listen carefully for a speaker's main ideas and points.	—	—
3. I take notes during meetings to keep a record of important information.	—	—
4. I am not often easily distracted.	—	—
5. I make an effort to keep my emotions under control.	—	—
6. I concentrate carefully and do not fake attention.	—	—
7. I wait for the speaker to finish speaking before I begin to evaluate what he has said.	—	—

The doors we open and close each day decide the lives we live.

8. I respond appropriately with a smile, a nod, or a word of acknowledgment (without disturbing other listeners) as a speaker is talking.   — —

9. I am aware of mannerisms that may distract a speaker and I try to keep mine under control.   — —

10. I am aware of and understand my biases and control them when I listen.   — —

11. I refrain from constantly interrupting.   — —

12. I value eye contact and maintain it most of the time.   — —

13. I often restate or paraphrase what the speaker said to make sure I have understood his intended meaning.   — —

14. I try to absorb the speaker's emotional meaning as well as subject matter content.   — —

15. I often ask questions for clarification.   — —

16. I do not finish other people's sentences unless I am asked to do so.   — —

17. When listening on the telephone, I keep one hand free to take notes.   — —

18. I attempt to set aside my ego and focus on the speaker and his message rather than on myself.   — —

"If you would like to be a power among man, cultivate enthusiasm."
Washington Irving

19. I make an effort to judge the message rather than the messenger. I understand that it's often easier to critize the information rather than to see how it may apply to me. __ __

20. I make an effort to be a patient listener. __ __

Scoring

1 — 5 *no*'s   You are an excellent listener.

6 — 10 *no*'s   You are a good listener, but can improve.

11 — 15 *no*'s   Through practice you can become a much more effective listener in your business and personal relationships.

16 — 20 *no*'s   Listen up!

This quiz has adapted from Diane Bone's *The Business of Listening*, published in Los Altos, California, by Crisp in 1988.

Working with Other People

Respect employees' feelings. Give yourself a *3* for always, a *2* for some of the time, a *1* for occasionally, a *0* for never.

__ I make an effort to greet each person pleasantly each day.

__ I take the time to manage by walking around, asking questions, chatting, and listening.

__ When I talk with employees, I make eye contact and speak respectfully and pleasantly.

__ I include others in as many decisions as possible.

__ I ask for others' advice on matters concerning their job, work area, etc.

"The heights by great men reached and kept, were not attained by sudden flight, but they, while their companions slept, were toiling upward in the night."
Henry Wadsworth Longfellow

___ I make an effort to treat everyone equally.

___ I do not knowingly withhold information from any team member or colleague.

___ I do not assign an overload without including essential employees in the decision-making process.

___ I emphasize team spirit and cooperation.

___ I do not assign special projects without carefully analyzing the growth needs of my employees and colleagues.

___ I praise in person when a job is well done.

___ I correct in private when a job is not well done.

___ I offer coaching and constructive suggestions to improve job performance and new skills.

___ I insist on high standards, exemplify those standards myself, and I communicate them respectfully.

___ Score.

This original version of this work quiz can be found in Twyla Dell's *An Honest Day's Work: Motivating Employees to Give Their Best,* published in Los Altos, California, by Crisp in 1988.

The Four-Step Management Meeting

Although they may have a job description and regular performance reviews, most workers unconsciously move away from the details they think their supervisors want them to do. Here is an effective plan that will correct this problem. Take a blank sheet of paper and complete the following exercises.

"To love is to believe, to hope to know,
it is a taste of heaven here below."

Waller

Five most important job functions:

1. _____

2. _____

3. _____

4. _____

5. _____

Write out your methods of achieving each of these job functions:

1. _____

2. _____

3. _____

4. _____

5. _____

Write out your goals to reach each of these job functions effectively:

1. _____

2. _____

3. _____

4. _____

5. _____

---

*The happiest people are those with achieving
experiences of helping others.*

Grade yourself as above average, average, or below average.

Now, ask your boss or that person reporting to you to do the same thing without seeing your sheet. Afterward, sit down together and compare notes with each other. You will find:

1. Unconsciously you have drifted apart. No one is at fault. It just happened.
2. You two can now take a third blank sheet and agree on your five most important job functions.
3. Have a checkup meeting once a month and stay on target.

The worker will feel better because he is on target with his boss. And the boss will be pleased because he will also know that the two of you are on target together.

In more than ninety-five percent of the cases, the boss rates the worker higher than the worker would rate him/herself. The reason: lack of supportive appreciation.

Team Building: Attitudes of an Effective Team Builder

By taking this quiz you can find your strengths and also your undeveloped areas in team building. On a scale of one to seven, circle the number that most closely corresponds to your evaluation of each question. Total the sum of the numbers when you have finished.

1. When I select employees, I choose those who can meet the job requirements and work well with others.

   7   6   5   4   3   2   1

2. I give employees a sense of ownership by involving them in goal-setting, problem-solving, and productivity-improvement activities.

   7   6   5   4   3   2   1

3. I try to provide team spirit by encouraging people to

"A happy family is but an earlier heaven."

Bowring

work together and to support one another on activities that are related.

7   6   5   4   3   2   1

4. I talk with people openly and honestly and encourage the same kind of communication in return.

7   6   5   4   3   2   1

5. I keep agreements with my people because their trust is essential to my leadership.

7   6   5   4   3   2   1

6. I help team members get to know each other so they can learn to trust, respect, and appreciate individual talent and ability.

7   6   5   4   3   2   1

7. I insure employees have the required training to do their job and know how it is to be applied.

7   6   5   4   3   2   1

8. I understand that conflict within groups is normal, but I work to resolve it quickly and fairly before it can become destructive.

7   6   5   4   3   2   1

9. I believe people will perform as a team when they know what is expected and what benefits will accrue.

7   6   5   4   3   2   1

10. I am willing to replace members who cannot or will not meet reasonable standards after appropriate coaching.

7   6   5   4   3   2   1

Total _____

A score of 60—70 indicates a positive attitude toward people and the type of attitude needed to build and maintain a strong team.

I've found that the way I treat others, determines the way they treat me.

A score of 40—59 is acceptable, and with reasonable effort, team building should be possible for you.

If you scored less than 40 points, you need to carefully examine your attitude in light of current management philosophy.

Listed here are thirty-one affirmations—one for each day of the month. Quote one each day, believe it, live it, and become it.

1. I accept myself totally and unconditionally.
2. I never devalue myself through destructive self-criticism.
3. I have warm, unconditional regard for myself and my friends.
4. I prove that I am alive by thinking, speaking, and acting with great enthusiasm.
5. I am completely self-determined about my future in my career.
6. I am an unusual, confident, achieving human being receiving an increasing flow of life's abundance.
7. I decide what thoughts will enter my mind.
8. I replace negative emotions with the opposite, positive emotions as the most effective way to take charge of my mind.
9. I keep only positive thoughts in my mind because they control what I will become.
10. I maintain complete control of my actions and emotions, thus sustaining my dynamic energies for worthwhile purposes.
11. My concept of life is constantly being enlarged as I seek beauty, health, wealth, joy, achievement, fulfillment, and happiness.
12. I enjoy all of life's experiences of fun, fellowship, laughter, and radiant joy.

Belief in heroics makes heroes.

13. Every day in every way, I am getting better and better.
14. My life is enriched since my activity is results-oriented.
15. I have true greatness still buried within me that is being released as my self-confidence, self-awareness, and self-appreciation expands.
16. I am the best friend I can have. I take myself out whenever I feel low. I alone am responsible for my feelings and I choose to feel beautiful.
17. I am a unique, never-to-be-repeated miracle of God. Therefore, today and every day, I celebrate myself.
18. Certainly I act differently, because I am different now that I control my thoughts.
19. I dwell on beautiful, powerful thoughts of self-affirmation.
20. I am forever free of negative thoughts such as doubt, fear, inferiority, hate, bitterness, strife, and hostility.
21. I live with the principle of unlimitedness. Abundance is mine because love, peace, joy, happiness, energy, health, and wealth have no boundaries.
22. I am energized by my newfound purpose, goals, dreams, and enthusiasm.
23. I welcome change and will ride the crest of new opportunities.
24. I am open, receptive, responsive, and obedient to life, love, joy, peace, energy, wealth, health, wisdom, and the beauty of wholeness.
25. I look for the good in all people.
26. I shall pass through this world but once. Any good, therefore, that I can do, or any kindness that I can show to any human being, let me do it now. Let me not defer or neglect it, because I shall not pass this way again.
27. A new friend is the best and most beautiful gift that I can give to myself.
28. I love other people unconditionally, as a result of my love for myself.

No one can make a fool of you unless you cooperate.

29. I will remember that the deepest urge of human nature is the desire to be important and I will sincerely and honestly seek to make every person I meet feel important.
30. The happiest people are those with achieving experiences of helping others.
31. I will give myself good feelings, diligent work, loyalty to my friends, and happy thoughts and I will thus assure myself high self-esteem.

Conclusion

My work is one of the finest expressions of who I am, therefore I will apply myself to the best of my ability to my work.

I will love my work. If I sincerely try and find myself not loving my work, I will seek other employment so that I can love what I do each and every day.

I will arrive at work excited and dedicated and will seek to produce more today than I did yesterday.

When I have felt depressed or discouraged,
it is because of the ways I let myself think and act.

CHAPTER 7

The Sacredness of Personhood

Originally, the word *guilt* came from a French word meaning *duty*. As with many other words, its usage has affected the meaning. Webster's now defines guilt as *fact of committing an offense, blameworthiness, feeling of responsibility for offense.*

Guilt may be used by controlling ministers, parents, or employers to make others feel bad. One of the worst things that we can do to ourselves is self-criticize and self-blame. This is done, so often, by negative, controlling words such as *ought*. By using *ought*, we are accepting others' control over us and our own self-blame.

How "oughts" often impact our lives:

I ought to be the perfect lover, friend, parent, or student.
I ought to be able to solve problems every time.
I ought to be able to handle any difficulty.
I ought never to feel bad, hurt, or negative.
I ought to be an outstanding achiever in everything I do.
I ought to anticipate every problem before it happens.
I ought never to feel anger, jealousy, or frustration.
I ought to love my children equally.
I ought to never make any mistakes.
I ought to be totally self-reliant at all times.
I ought never to have to ask anyone else how to do things.
I ought never to get tired or sick.
I ought never to be afraid.
I ought to be such an achiever that I will be wealthy.

I ought to be busy at all times and never take time out for myself.

I ought to be the best at my job.

I ought to be kind to all people even when I don't feel like being kind.

I ought to feel sexually excited about my mate at all times.

I ought to care about the poor and homeless.

I ought to be able to make enough money for my family to have all they need.

I ought to be able to protect my children from all fears and pain.

I ought to never take time for myself, but work always.

With these guilt-loaded thoughts, you have surrendered your control to fear, insecurity, and negative emotions.

Instead, take the positive approach by making your life a choice:

I choose to be the best lover, friend, parent, or student.

I choose to anticipate and solve all problems to the best of my ability.

I choose to handle all difficulties to the best of my abilities.

I choose to put my negative emotions and hurts into positive emotions.

I choose to be an outstanding achiever in all that I do.

I choose to feel anger, jealousy, or frustration when they are deserved.

I choose to love my children unconditionally and like them according to their conduct.

I choose to admit my mistakes and not blame myself for them, but learn from them.

I choose to be self-reliant to the best of my ability.

I choose to maintain good health, although sometimes I may get sick.

"If a child lives with approval, he learns to like himself."
Dorothy Law Nolte

I choose not to be overwhelmed by fear, but admit sometimes I have fears.

I choose to be the best at my job, because I like myself better when I do.

I choose to be kind to all people when I possibly can.

I choose to feel sexually excited about my mate whenever possible.

I choose to care for the poor and homeless and help them as I can.

I choose to make the money necessary to provide for my family.

I choose to protect my children from fear and pain as best I can.

I choose to work hard and enjoy my leisure equally as well.

Ought living is wrong, especially when it is employed with controlling, emotionally abusive conduct. To demand ought-motivated behavior as part of a person's conduct violates the sacredness of personhood. If you allow for *choice* conduct, individuals have the opportunity to freely make moral decisions regarding themselves and their actions.

Your Choice Inventory

I choose to maintain relationships: mate, children, parents, siblings, friends, etc.

I choose activities: cleaning, working, playing, cooking, hobbies, etc.

I choose recreational and social activities: dining out, vacations, weekends out-of-town, fishing, gardening, hunting, games, exercise, etc.

I choose good work habits: being on time, doing my best, loyalty to my company, learning, growing, improving, earning a raise, earning a promotion, etc.

"In all things we learn from those we love."

Goethe

I choose creative activities: church, clubs, reading, selective TV viewing, spirited discussions, traveling, etc.

I choose money and financial success: saving, investing, living on a budget, planning for retirement, etc.

I choose self-care: good appearance/dress, exercise, control intake of drugs, not smoking, careful eating habits, dieting when necessary, pride in myself, etc.

I choose ways of expression: anger, fear, love, affection, joy, sexual pleasure, controlling physical pain, etc.

In 1924, at the Olympics, Charles Pollock won a silver medal in the hundred-meter dash. In the early 1930s, Pollock was speaking at a high school in Cleveland. A skinny, fourteen-year-old boy came up to Pollock after his speech and said, "Mr. Pollock, I will do anything to win an Olympic medal." Pollock reached into his pocket and handed that boy an Olympic coin and said, "If you will pay the price of total commitment, you can win it. Take this coin as a sign of that commitment." In 1936, in Berlin, that boy, Jessie Owen, won four gold medals, including one for setting a world's record in the hundred-meter dash.

A few years later, speaking at East High in Cleveland, Jessie Owen was greeted after his talk by a tall, skinny boy. He said, "Mr. Owen, I will do anything to win a gold medal in the Olympics." Owen reached into his pocket and took out that same Olympic coin that Charles Pollock had given him some years before, and said, "Charles Pollock gave me this medal as my inspiration many years ago. I want you to have it with your commitment that you will pay the price of greatness." That boy, Harrison ("Bones") Dillard, won the high jump and a gold medal in the 1948 Olympics at London.

Three great athletes, all with high self-esteem, passed on the torch of greatness.

I am a unique, never-to-be-repeated miracle of God.
Therefore, today and everyday, I celebrate myself.

A professional speaker, a friend of mine, went to Silver City, New Mexico, to speak at a chamber of commerce banquet. During dinner, he turned to the man on his right and asked, "How is business?"

The man answered, "I am a real-estate broker with my own office. The two silver mines here have been out on strike for six months. I haven't sold a house in that time. If this strike lasts three months more, I will be broke. This is the worst time of my life," he complained.

The speaker turned to the woman on his left and asked her, "How's business?"

She excitedly replied, "I'm in real estate. This strike will be settled soon and all the workers for the mining companies will receive a good raise. Before the strike, the miners who work a lot of overtime haven't had the time to look for houses. Now they have plenty of time. I have sold more houses in the last six months than any three years in my life. I hope the strike ends soon, but if it lasts another three months, I will be set for life. Business is the best I have ever seen."

Here were two people, three feet apart. One, the woman, with high self-esteem, was making lemonade out of a lemon. The man was strangling on his lemon. He had low self-esteem.

What you believe about yourself makes all the difference in the world for you and those around you. We treat other people in the same way that we feel about ourselves. If you have genuine self-esteem, you can practice life's greatest ability: the ability to get along with people. Use these human relations rules:

Show genuine interest in the other person.
Smile. It spreads like a wildfire. You smile; others will also.
Be sure you get the other person's name. Use it, remember it,

---

There is more pleasure in loving than in being loved.

and recall it later. Dale Carnegie said, "The sweetest sound in any language is the sound of our own name."

Listen to all the other person says. Encourage him to talk about himself.

Talk about what he is interested in. Keep the ball in his court.

Make other people feel important. Make them feel you really care.

Give sincere compliments. Compliment people on things about their personalities, abilities, attitudes, etc. Everyone has something you can positively compliment him/her on. Look for good things people do and express your appreciation. They will rise up and call you blessed.

Never criticize. It puts others on the defensive and does no good. Use corrective suggestions for overcoming a mistake. Speak to someone privately. Call attention to some of your own mistakes, compliment a person on other achievements he has made and then ask, "Could this have been handled in some other way?" Together, you both can correct the mistake. He will feel good about it, will appreciate you on the way you have handled it, and will make a much better effort the next time.

Learn to accept compliments. Accept them, and thank the other person for them. Never reject the compliment. That offends the other person and makes you feel unworthy.

Talk little about yourself. Don't tell what *you* have done, etc.

Be pleasant. Enjoy what you are doing. If you don't like your job, either change your attitude or change your job. Don't say, "I have to go to work today." Instead, say, "I choose to go to work today, because I choose to pay my bills." Smell the roses.

As a guide on how to be assertive, not aggressive or recessive, the following lists may be helpful:

When love and skill work together, expect a masterpiece.

Assertive Behavior

Sensitive to feelings
Needs no threats
Force used only when and where necessary
Based on human rights
Firm but gentle, unyielding where appropriate
Negotiation a viable tactic
Leads to good feelings
Accepts workable outcomes

Aggressive Behavior

Insensitive to feelings
Attack-oriented
Use of force or threats of force
Leads to frustration and guilt
Either victory or defeat, no middle ground
Anger
Demands preconceived outcomes
Uses people

Recessive Behavior

Insensitive to needs and desires
Yields too often
Sacrifices basic human rights
Accepts unwanted outcomes
Leads to frustration, guilt, and bad feelings
Feel used and manipulated

Your Rights

Right to say "no" without feeling guilty
Right to make choices
Right to agree or disagree
Right to take care of yourself
Right to have your say

To love is to place our happiness in the care of another.

Right to ask for help
Right to reject
Right to change your mind

Positive Statements

"He who fails to prepare prepares to fail." Preparation is a key element in success. Preparation gives one the self-confidence that he/she is ready to meet a challenge.

Good things don't happen because one hopes for them. They happen because of positive actions.

A positive attitude is like an umbrella — it keeps you from getting all wet.

Technical knowledge becomes outdated every three years on the average, but positive attitudes will last you for a lifetime. Acquire the positive attitudes that can help you cope with change.

"Whatever you vividly imagine, ardently desire, sincerely believe and enthusiastically act upon — must inevitably come to pass." (Paul Meyer)

The best accessory you can add to any wardrobe is a smile.

To catch the big fish, you must be in the deep water; to accomplish great things you must be willing to leave the security of shallow water and venture where the water is deep and maybe where you have never been before.

A positive person realizes that in order for him to "win," someone else doesn't have to lose. In fact, the best way to win is to help someone else win.

Smile to let others know you are there. Smile to let them know you care. Soon there will be smiles everywhere.

The best attitude to have towards one's daily work is a keep-at-it-tude.

A positive person knows that it is better to have done something imperfectly while giving 100-percent effort than to have done nothing perfectly while giving no effort.

"For as he thinketh in his heart, so is he. . . ."

Prov. 23:7

There should be no shame in admitting that you were wrong—instead be proud you are strong enough to admit a mistake, and be glad that you are wiser from having learned from your mistake or error.

Every man's work is a portrait of himself. Put your best effort into everything you do and your work will be a positive reflection of the kind of person you are.

A person who takes shortcuts usually finds himself on a dead-end street. Positive people know there are no shortcuts to success. It takes preparation, hard work, and dedication to be successful.

Keep in mind a positive thought. . . . attitudes are learned and can be taught.

You never fail unless you fail to learn from your mistakes.

You can try your best and make the best of everything.

A person is as young as his dreams—or as old as his doubts. Let your dreams rule your life—not your doubts.

Abraham Lincoln once said, "People are as happy as they make up their minds to be." Develop the habit of being happy.

Everyone has the potential to be a winner. The seeds of greatness are inside each of us.

Benjamin Franklin said, "If a man empties his purse into his head, no man can take it away from him. An investment in knowledge always pays the best interest."

Each new day is a new beginning. Claim your positive potential for greatness.

Be resolved to make this a positive year for yourself. Think positively, act positively, and become a positive person.

A positive person knows that great minds discuss events, small minds discuss people.

Smile, because as Sir Isaac Newton would say, "Every action has a reaction." If you smile, people will react positively.

Every goal has a beginning, a middle, and an end. So just by beginning to accomplish a goal, you are one-third of the way toward accomplishing your goal.

Home is a happy haven from harm.

Shakespeare said, "Our doubts are traitors and make us lose the good we oft might win by fearing to attempt." Don't let the fear of failure control your life. If you want something, go for it. Give it a 110-percent effort and you will have nothing to fear.

Thinking and looking negative will only bring you down. So put on a smile and get rid of your frown.

A positive person knows that not everything faced can be changed, but that nothing can be changed until it is faced. So face those things which interfere with your progress, or stand in the way of a goal you have, and try to change them.

All things work for the best for those who make the best of everything. You can become a positive person by thinking and acting positively each day.

An attitude is like a bread roll—when it goes stale and flat, it's not worth having around.

Enthusiasm is not reserved for only a fortunate few. Anyone and everyone can become an enthusiastic person by practicing being enthusiastic. It will become a good habit which will open many doors for you.

Pull the plug on negative thoughts and let them go down the drain.

Only in math does negative times negative equal positive.

Think not negative thoughts for they bring you lower in self-pride, but if you think positive thoughts they'll lift you higher than you imagine.

Be a positive person, go an extra mile.

Ten Commandments of the Lovable, Liberated Man

1. Thou shalt feel free to openly express your emotions honestly.
2. Thou shalt be open to honor and respect logical, practical, and intellectual viewpoints with thy mate.

We shall pass this way but once, so celebrate life to the fullest.

3. Thou shalt listen and value what is said both mentally and emotionally.
4. Thou shalt appreciate women as equals.
5. Thou shalt mutually share, experience, and explore the pleasures of sensuality.
6. Thou shalt recognize and encourage healthy ego growth equally with thy mate.
7. Thou shalt recognize thy partner as equal breadwinner to thyself if she so chooses.
8. Thou shalt share responsibility for housework with thy mate, especially if she works.
9. Thou shalt openly achieve vocational excellence that gives you personal satisfaction.
10. Thou shalt mutually seek the answer to problems of common interest.

What are some of the things men fear so much?

Men fear sexual failure. And when they are selfish in their lovemaking rather than sharing their total selves, they tend to have more problems with sexual achievement.

Men are afraid of aggressive women. This is because they don't know how to handle them. An aggressive woman should not be a threat, but this drive should be channeled into effective productivity that benefits everyone.

Men are afraid of a passive, nonresponsive woman. This is because they have not learned the art of arousing such a woman to her real potential.

Men are afraid of rejection. They are looking for someone else to meet their own emotional needs rather than learning to meet these needs within themselves.

Men are afraid of competing with a woman. Such a person is insecure, because competition should be a challenge to excellence.

Love people and use things, not love things and use people.

Men are afraid of female competence. They have been taught that women are basically inferior, which isn't true.

Men are afraid of failure. Often this is because they haven't developed genuine self-esteem.

Learning to Love

Becoming a lovable, liberated person. To become a lovable, liberated person, you must repudiate guilt, because most of it comes from things, which are not wrong as much as they are taught to be wrong by controlling, insecure parents and by fear-imposing, negative religion.

Looking at the ineffective roles we have been taught, we find:

The Limited Female

1. She has a poor self-image, either not developed in her home by her parents, or she has failed to develop her self-esteem because of a husband who puts her down, or just the role of male-superior vs. female-inferior syndrome.
2. She doesn't value her body, mind, and abilities.
3. She maintains a Puritanical attitude toward sex.
4. She is guilt-ridden.
5. She has an unreasonable fear of change.
6. She sits on her feelings, then explodes.
7. She has few hobbies, personal interests, or things that she enjoys doing.

The Limited Male

1. He has a poor self-image. He is unhappy in his work, dresses with poor taste, and is emotionally withdrawn.
2. He is filled with a fear of rejection.

"Happy are the families where the government of parents is the reign of affection."

Francis Bacon

3. He has a low tolerance for others. He is frustrated and hates to wait for anyone.
4. He is loaded with guilt.
5. He holds strong prejudices.
6. He is selfish with his love. He can't say, "I love you."

Why can't men show their feelings—especially express their love to their wives and children?

1. Some have used love words to seduce women and therefore feel guilty in using them with ones close to them.
2. They never experienced such endearments in their homes from their parents and thus don't feel comfortable with them.
3. Some feel such expressions would mean they would be emotionally untrue to their mothers by telling other women they love them. These men fail to understand the paradox of love, for the more a man loves his mother, the greater capacity he has to love his children, and the greater capacity he has to love his wife.
One man hadn't kissed his wife in twenty years, and then shot another man for doing it. He is the one who should have been shot.
4. Saying "I love you" is uncomfortable for some men, for they harbor an unconscious hostility towards women.
5. Others think that emotional expression is a final and complete letting go, and they don't know how to do so. You see, they aren't in control of their unused and unfamiliar emotions.
6. Some men think that loving is destructive to their sense of freedom and independence. Truly, such persons are in a prison of emotional constipation.
7. Some men think it isn't masculine to show emotions. Of course, such a person is more robotic than manly.

I can change my life by taking charge of my emotions.

8. If a man thinks sex is dirty, then he associates words of tenderness with vulgarity and obscenity.
9. And, finally, this type of man is afraid that tenderness is a total surrender of logic to emotion.

What is the answer? Let's look at the qualities of the lovable, liberated person.

The Lovable, Liberated Woman

1. She and her man come first in her life. Everyone knows she cares.
2. She is open, honest, and frank in conversation. She gets it out, forgives, and forgets. She never denies sex in revenge.
3. She initiates and lets him lead. She has the attitude, "If you ask me, I'll say yes." She is not fearful, but trusting.
4. She enjoys and encourages the beautiful pleasure of sex. She knows that most men have a limited knowledge of sexual matters; that the refusal of sex is a total rejection of a man; that a lack of femininity is an attack on his manhood; that her mate loves others to admire her as an extension of his personhood. He is saying, "Hey, look but don't touch." And she knows that men really respond to affection.
5. She realizes that men have a low tolerance for stress and frustration. She doesn't make him wait for an unreasonable length of time.
6. She accepts his interest in sports. She knows that "the difference between men and boys is the size of their toys."
7. She knows men detest being manipulated by guilt and martyrdom. She doesn't bitch.
8. She accepts his dedication to his work. She helps him

I live in the principle of unlimitedness. Abundance is mine for love, peace, joy, happiness, energy, health, wealth know no boundaries.

achieve balance by making his leisure time as exciting and meaningful as his work.

9. She knows that few people can resist emotional involvement with someone who really cares.

10. She loves herself, so out of the overflow of her self-celebration she abundantly loves him.

11. She has developed such genuine self-esteem through her work, social life, or other activity that she meets her own emotional needs, and thus isn't burdening him to meet her needs.

The Lovable, Liberated Man

1. He has genuine self-esteem and is not threatened by job loss, financial difficulties, family conflicts, or even the loss of love.

2. He is equally partnered to love his mate and children as much as his work.

3. He is a lifelong student of the art of love. He is curious about learning every way to help his mate enjoy their love life more. He is turned on by emotions, words, experiences, as well as his mate's appearance.

4. He is open and honest about his feelings. He loves to express his warmth and affection for her and does it without reason and as an act of his fullness.

5. He wants his mate to be mature and happy, and he is not threatened by her achievements.

6. He wants to regularly enjoy exciting leisure activities with his mate and children.

7. He can read and adjust to his mate's emotional wavelengths.

8. He is not a mama's boy in that he is controlled by his mother. He has equal love for his mother, his mate, and his children. He is his own man and will never let his mother separate him from his mate.

---

*The greatest use of life is to so live your life
that the use of your life outlives your life.*

9. He delights in his partner's freedom, personhood, happiness, and individuality.
10. He accepts and cultivates her leisure activity as important to her personhood, and thus their happiness.
11. He makes her financially secure so that she will never be threatened by the worry of financial destitution were she to lose him.

The Ideal Lovable, Liberated Person

1. He is assertive, assured, and confident.
2. He has willpower and is balanced emotionally and logically.
3. He is free to express himself emotionally and is able to laugh and cry.
4. He has genuine self-esteem, self-confidence, self-value, and self-celebration.
5. He is a loving, warm, tender, and sensuous person, because to live a life without sexual fulfillment is to accept punishment without cause.
6. He is strong, decisive, and in control of himself.
7. He is excited about life, people, and especially his mate and children.
8. He is cooperative and eager to build a relationship for a lifetime.
9. He puts himself first, so the overflow of joy will spill over on all who are touched.
10. He is a growing, searching, and fulfilled individual who is excited by life's fantastic opportunities.

Conclusion

In order to be whole yourself, you must go back and heal the harmful experiences you have had with others. Pray for those you

---

*"Success can only be measured by mastering
fundamentals, developing physical and mental toughness,
hard work, and making the second effort."*
Vince Lombardi

have injured. Then, after a time of conditioning your mind to harmony, go to those persons and offer your peace. Not everyone will not respond positively. Those that don't, forget them. You know in your heart that you have made your peace. You will be at peace within yourself. That's what counts. The ones who do respond positively will bring you a joy that will fill your heart.

Establish as a condition of life that you will never criticize another person. Look for the good in others. With kind words of praise and appreciation, you can bring out that good and both of you will enjoy warm feelings of good will.

Remember that life's greatest ability is the ability to get along well with other people. You do this by making them feel important. The greatest drive of every person is to feel important.

---

*"The deepest urge of human nature is the desire
to be and feel important."*

William James

CHAPTER 8

Rewriting Your Tape: Why Did America's No. 1 Box Office Attraction Quit the Movies?

In 1965, at the height of her movie career, number one female box office star, Kim Novak, walked away from Hollywood and moved to the Big Sur, "running to my life."

Kim never felt that she was special as a child. "Oh, how I miss the fact that I never heard 'I love you' from [my parents]. It's something that I longed for, that keeps me always feeling that I never had enough love."

Her parents were strict Catholics and severe disciplinarians. They instilled in her the belief that she was very fragile and vulnerable. She felt she had to prove her worth; she sought her father's approval but never felt that she ever earned it, not matter how hard she worked for it.

"My father could never get in touch with his feelings or talk about them. He was remote, very private, a loner, raised in a family of farmers who believed in hard, physical work."

Her father, Joseph Novak, worked for the Chicago-Milwaukee Railroad and raised Kim and her sister in a tough, working-class district of Chicago where she was a shy, often frightened child with few friends.

Kim worked with a lot of powerful men in Hollywood— Harry Cohn, Otto Preminger, and Alfred Hitchcock. They were like her father, for she felt that she could never gain their approval.

"Yes, I felt like I was coming home." Kim was named the most popular star in the world in 1956, only two years after the release of her first movie. Kim was asked what went wrong. Why did she leave such an exalted position?

She felt she was sinking. "All I wanted was for them to tell me that I was doing something right, to let me find some way that I could be good." She tells how when she first went into show business, she had a pact with God, that she wanted to serve him and to do something meaningful. She says she had never really wanted to be an actor until it happened. "I thought, 'God thinks enough of me to let me communicate to the whole world.' I took it very seriously, and then as time went on, it [her life] seemed to be slipping through my fingers."

And what happened after she withdrew from the Hollywood scene? "I made nature my parents, my teachers. My teachers became the animals, the plants, the sea."

In 1974, nine years after leaving Hollywood, Kim met Dr. Robert Malloy, a veterinarian. Now they have been happily married for twenty years. Kim became her own self-nurturing parent. She discovered her self-value, her self-esteem.

If your parents did not raise you to have high self-esteem, then you must become your own self-nurturing parent and discover your own sense of importance. That's the way to wholeness.

How to Rate Your Self-Esteem

(Answer True or False.)

___ 1. I usually feel inferior to other people.

___ 2. I feel that I am a warm, loving and happy person.

"A relationship is a loving thing. It needs and benefits from the same attention an artist lavishes on his art."

David Viscott

F 3. When things go wrong, I usually say, "Just my luck."

F 4. I feel life is wonderful and I can make it.

I 5. I have a strong drive to prove myself.

F 6. I am free of guilt, fear, and negative emotions.

I 7. I have a strong desire for recognition and approval.

F 8. I don't need to correct other people's mistakes.

I 9. When things don't work out right, I feel like a loser.

I 10. I look forward to new opportunities with enthusiasm.

E 11. I feel I must correct other people when they go wrong.

I 12. I do my own thinking and make my own decisions.

I 13. I tend to be critical and belittling of other people.

I 14. I am confident in meeting my own needs and reaching my goals.

I 15. I tend to sell my talents, abilities, and accomplishments short.

I 16. I am usually poised and confident around strangers.

I 17. I am vulnerable to the opinions and criticism of others.

I 18. I bear no prejudice toward people of other races or ethnic backgrounds.

I 19. I am fearful of revealing who I really am.

Two or more minds agreed in perfect harmony create a super mind, greater than the totality of the individual minds.

___ 20. I feel comfortable with myself and enjoy times of being alone.

___ 21. I am a compulsive "perfectionist."

___ 22. I accept compliments graciously and with appreciation.

___ 23. I am often compulsive in eating, talking, and drinking.

___ 24. I am appreciative of other people's accomplishments and talents.

___ 25. I don't like new experiences because I feel I will fail.

___ 26. I easily make new friends and keep old friends.

___ 27. I feel uneasy making new friends, because many people are not sincere.

___ 28. I easily admit my mistakes, because I learn from them.

___ 29. It is very important to me that people approve of me.

___ 30. I accept my responsibility to meet my own emotional needs.

___ 31. I often am embarrassed by the actions of some of my friends.

___ 32. I can accept someone's "put-down" without taking offense.

___ 33. It is very important to me for my boss to give me compliments.

---

*"Flaming enthusiasm, backed up by horse sense and
persistence, is the quality that most frequently makes for success."*
Dale Carnegie

__1__ 34. I judge my self-worth by comparing myself to others.

Scoring

15 — 17 *true* answers to the odd statements and 15 — 17 *false* answers to the even statements mean you have very low self-esteem. (16)

10 — 14 *true* answers to the odd statements and 10 — 14 *false* answers to the even statements mean you have low self-esteem. (4)

5 — 9 *true* answers to the odd statements and 5 — 9 *false* answers to the even statements mean you have average self-esteem.

10 — 14 *false* answers to the odd statements and 10 — 14 *true* answers to the even statements mean you have high self-esteem.

15 — 17 *false* answers to the odd statements and 15 — 17 *true* answers to the even statements mean you have very high self-esteem.

My Childhood Role Models

	Father	Mother	Sister	Brother	Other
1. Attitude toward myself	____	____	____	____	____
2. Attitude toward men	____	____	____	____	____
3. Attitude toward women	____	____	____	____	____
4. Attitude about work	____	____	____	____	____
5. Attitude about emotions	____	____	____	____	____
6. Who played criticizer?	____	____	____	____	____
7. Who played victim?	____	____	____	____	____
8. Who played goof-off?	____	____	____	____	____
9. Who played irresponsible?	____	____	____	____	____
10. Who played peacemaker?	____	____	____	____	____

If you work hard enough, and smart enough, success is sure to follow.

11. Who played pessimist?   ____ ____ ____ ____ ____
12. Who held the power?   ____ ____ ____ ____ ____
13. Who played optimist?   ____ ____ ____ ____ ____
14. Who played official
     worrier?   ____ ____ ____ ____ ____
15. Who played achiever?   ____ ____ ____ ____ ____
16. Who played the clown?   ____ ____ ____ ____ ____
17. Who played out of sorts?   ____ ____ ____ ____ ____
18. Who was the "heavy"?   ____ ____ ____ ____ ____
19. Who manipulated whom?   ____ ____ ____ ____ ____
20. Who was scared most of
     the time?   ____ ____ ____ ____ ____
21. Who was happy?   ____ ____ ____ ____ ____
22. Whose values
     predominated?   ____ ____ ____ ____ ____
23. Whom did you pattern
     after?   ____ ____ ____ ____ ____
24. Whom did you reject?   ____ ____ ____ ____ ____

In re-evaluating this role model, you can determine who influenced your life the most and choose to relate to the ones whose positive models you choose.

Remember, self-esteem is that package of beliefs about yourself that you carry around inside, and which you take for granted is the real truth about yourself, whether it is or not.

If you rated low on the self-esteem test, you must rewrite your script, or tape, so that you can develop genuine self-esteem.

You can also view self-esteem as the self-accepted reputation you have with yourself, but a reputation and the real truth are often different.

People with low self-esteem are the ones who are both the victor and the victim in the *fatal attraction* syndrome. There are three stages of this kind of romantic love:

Stage I: The Fantasy Stage. The emotion is loneliness, the

The destiny of my life is up to me.

dynamic is hope. The fantasy is to find someone to meet my needs. Since I am incomplete without love, then I will be complete when I have met the ideal love of my life. There is a fantastic attraction when two people, both desperate for love, meet. Each one's own desperate chemistry hooks into the desperate chemistry of the other person.

The infatuation is a match with the mental role model I so desperately need. The energy is powerful. The sex is overwhelming. It is an infantile, unfulfilled need that craves satisfaction. The script is to find someone to "feel bad" with. The next day, or in a few days, the questions come: "If this love is so great, when am I going to feel better? Why isn't this person meeting my needs?" The truth is, the other person can't meet your needs, for the other person can't meet his own needs. And you don't know what your own needs are. Manipulation follows. You must force this person to meet your needs. So you start controlling the other person. Criticism and conflict follow.

The symptoms are as follows:

1. Primarily physical
2. Strong sex appeal
3. Little or no rational involvement
4. You hurt deeply when you are away from him/her
5. Lots of argument, frustration, and conflict when you are together
6. Your children and friends often can't understand what you see in this person
7. Usually you together have few value relationships
8. Both have probably been through a number of such experiences
9. Very little mental control

This affair will most likely break up in a short time. Most do. Then you feel hurt, cheated, that you are a failure,

---

Definiteness of purpose is the starting point of all achievement.

angry, and resentful toward the other person. As often as eight hundred times a day, thoughts of the other person flood your memory. This is the time when one may kill the other. The reason is not just anger toward the other person, but anger toward life. For a part of yourself, the incomplete, troubled, desperate self is even more fractured than before. *When the other person left, he took a part of you.* After all, Hollywood and the great music themes have promised that love is the answer to all needs. This lie has become truth to a great number of desperate people.

Get into counseling. Stay away from the other person. Throw yourself into your work and other constructive activities. The other person is not the reason. Don't blame him. He is just as hurt as you.

Stage II: The Anxiety Stage. The emotion is pain. The dynamic is power. You feel if you could force the other person to fulfill his obligation to you, it would work out. This whole problem comes from the script you have been living with.

A bad script comes with these feelings:

1. I am not wanted.
2. I blame myself, my parents, others, etc.
3. It's all my fault.
4. I'm not enough.
5. I'm powerless.
6. I'm not good enough.
7. I'm a failure because I wouldn't please my parents, others, etc.
8. I can be perfect.

Usually this bad script comes from a home where the

"Enthusiasm is the mother of effort and without it nothing great was ever accomplished."
Ralph Waldo Emerson

parents and other adults, by their criticism, had contributed to your low self-esteem. So, you live an illusion.

Signs of an illusion include:

1. You are looking for a perfect mate.
2. You feel unlovable and unworthy.
3. You want to be loved more than to love.
4. You fear if you find love it won't be enough.
5. You want to be loved before you will give any love back.
6. You believe there is only one person in the world to meet your needs.
7. You look for someone to trust you before you will open up.
8. You continually fantasize with false expectations.
9. You are looking for someone to care about you, but you are unable to care back.
10. You believe love will solve all problems including loneliness.
11. You keep searching for someone to love rather than becoming a loving person.
12. You blame yourself for being alone.
13. You don't realize that affection is shared in many ways.
14. You feel you have never been loved by your parents.
15. You think that love is only an emotion.

How to get over this stage and become a real person:

1. You must determine the script and change it. Usually must have counseling. Few people can find their own bad scripts and change them.
2. You must rewrite the bad script into a good script. This is healing.
3. You must develop high self-esteem. Must learn to accept yourself, value yourself, and learn to love yourself.

You can change your life by changing your attitudes or mind.

4. You must develop own pathway to growth and pursue it as a lifelong journey.
5. You must work through to reality.

You must realize that love is not an emotion, or an energy. Love is a learned response. Love is a decision to act in a loving, caring manner. Love is a commitment to your own growth and happiness and a commitment to the safety, satisfaction, security, and happiness of the person loved. Love is a decision not to criticize the other person. Love is a pattern to live your life in harmony, happiness, unity, and sharing life's great moments. Love is a commitment to grow to become the kind of person you always have wanted to become. Love is encouraging the one loved to become all he/she can become.

How do you know when you are in reality? When you can positively write out ten things about yourself you want to improve, can sit down and discuss this openly with another person, and honestly agree on a plan of action to grow.

Stage III: Real Love. The emotion is serenity, the dynamic is sharing love. Now you can share love rationally as a fact. You can share love emotionally as a feeling and behaviorally as an act. You are a totally self-accepting individual. You are living in the truth of your healthy selfhood. You are the supplier of your own emotional needs. You have decided to love yourself.

Keys to Genuine Self-Esteem

The secret to inner peace lies in self-affirmation, a quiet celebration.

You can't change others, but you can change your reactions to others.

"There is no man, no woman, so small but that they cannot make their life great by high endeavor."
Thomas Carlyle

The path to inner peace requires awareness, courage, decision, and action.

Form a positive personal belief system that values and celebrates yourself.

In your internal cast of characters, the troublemakers will be your "not OK" and "critical parent" tapes. They are hooked into the love of power. They try to manipulate, control, and win. Your nurturing adult and natural child are concerned with the power of love. They are the ones that work for the best interest of you and others.

To increase your self-worth, you do not need to change yourself. You need to change your "self-talk" and your negative beliefs about yourself. You can choose to become your own nurturing parent.

Change the words "should," ought," "must," "have to," to those of the nurturing parent—"wish," "prefer," "want," "choose," "feel," and "desire."

You can choose not to react to the judgments of others. You do this by giving space to blame but refusing to take their bait.

Reasonable expectations are nurturing. Unreasonable ones cause pain.

When you are upset, check what expectations have gone unmet.

Your inner criticizer will ask for perfection in feelings, thoughts, and deeds. Give yourself permission to be less than perfect. Do not cling to past mistakes, but rather release them.

Give up the belief that things should always go as you want them to. Others don't have to match your feelings, attitudes, and values. Life and others are not expected to know how you feel or what you want without being told.

Take time for meaningful pleasure. Put balance into your life by doing those things that give you release from the pressures of daily work.

"Some people regard discipline as a chore.
For me it is a kind of order that sets me free to fly."
Julie Andrews

Improve your family, business, and friend relationships. We draw strength from the positive people around us. Release negative relationships that are destructive to your own feelings.

Write out goals for your life — career, family, personal, and professional goals. If you fail to plan, you are planning to fail.

With subliminal videocassettes and audiotapes, condition yourself to positive self-talk. You alone are responsible for your feelings. Impact yourself with affirmations that give you the feelings and assurances of success.

After Ty Cobb retired from baseball, he became a scout for the Detroit Tigers. He was sent to Memphis to check out a twenty-one-year-old first baseman. He returned after three days to Detroit and said, "Forget him. He's as clumsy as an ox in the field and he can't hit curve balls."

Three years later, that player, Lou Gehrig, was the first baseman for the New York Yankees. The Detroit management said to Cobb, "Ty, you missed that one."

"No," said Ty. Somewhere within those three years, Gehrig decided to pay the *price of greatness.* Lou Gehrig had high self-esteem.

Andy Strasberg is the director of marketing for the San Diego Padres. He says, "I went to my first baseball game as an 8-year-old. My dad took me to the Giants-Phillies game. I fell in love with baseball.

"In 1960, Roger Maris came to the Yankees from Kansas City. That year, Roger won the most valuable player award. He became my idol. In 1961, the entire country was wrapped up in the home run race between Maris and Mickey Mantle and Babe Ruth's ghost. I cut out every single article on Roger and eight years later, had them bound in an eleven-volume scrapbook.

"We work to become, not to acquire."
Elbert Hubbard

"I always sat in Section 31, Row 162-A, Seat 1 in Yankee Stadium. Right field. I would watch Maris park his car and told him what a big fan I was. After awhile, he began to notice me. He threw me a baseball in batting practice. I was so excited, I couldn't lift my arms to catch it. Someone else got it. I yelled to Roger that I didn't get it, so he stopped and gave me another one.

"My friends kept pushing me to ask Roger for one of his bats. He said, 'Sure, next time I break the bat.' That was 1965. When the team was in Los Angeles, I heard on the radio that Roger had broken his bat.

"When the team returned to New York, during batting practice, Roger came over to me and gave me his bat and said, 'I've got this bat for you.'

"I said, 'Oh, my God, I can't thank you enough.' He knew who I was. He had brought that bat back from L.A.

"I brought that bat home and told my friends. They said, 'Now that you have the bat, why not ask him for one of his home run balls.'

"I asked Roger for one. He said, 'You're gonna have to catch one 'cause I don't have any.'

"Maris was traded to St. Louis on December 8, 1966. In 1967, while in school at the University of Akron in Ohio, one day six of us drove to Pittsburgh to see Roger play the Pirates. I saw Roger as he was entering the stadium. I went up to him and said, 'Roger.'

"He turned and said, 'Andy Strasberg, what the hell are you doing here in Pittsburgh?' That was the first time I knew that Roger knew my name.

"I replied, 'Well, I'm here with some guys from college and we wanted to say hello.'

"I introduced my friends to Roger. Roger said, 'Wait a minute, I want to give you an autographed National League ball.' I felt like a million dollars.

You get the best out of others when you give the best of yourself.

"That day, I sat in Row 9, Seat 9 out in right field. In the third inning, Roger hit a home run off Woodie Fryman. I caught the ball. The most amazing thing in the world had happened to me. Tears were rolling down my face. When Roger came to right field he looked up at me and said, 'I can't believe it.'

"I said, 'You can't, I can't.'

"Back at school, I was afraid I was going to lose that baseball, so I went down to the Akron Dime National Bank and put it in a safety deposit box. Later, when I was back in New York, Roger came to Shea Stadium and Roger signed that ball. In 1968, Roger played his last game in St. Louis. I flew out to see him play. I was seated behind the dugout. When Roger came into the dugout, he stopped, saw me in the stands and winked at me. A reporter for *Sporting News* saw that and interviewed me. When he found out I had flown out from New York to see Roger's last game, the reporter asked Roger about me and Roger said, 'Andy Strasberg was my most loyal fan.'

"Roger and I started exchanging Christmas cards and the relationship continued. When I got the job with the Padres, Roger wrote me a letter of congratulations. When I got married in 1976, Rog and his wife, Pat, sent us a wedding gift, and we talked on the phone several times a year. In 1980, when Roger and Pat were in Los Angeles for the All-Star Game, we (my wife, Patti; my dad; Roger and Pat) went out to dinner.

"Roger passed away in December 1985. I made arrangements to go to Fargo, North Dakota, for the services. After the services, I went up to Pat. She hugged me, introduced me to their six children and said, 'I want to introduce you to someone really special, kids; this is Andy Strasberg.'

"I have yet to find the man, however exalted his station,
who did not do better work and put forth greater effort
under a spirit of approval, than under a spirit of criticism."
Charles Schwab

"Roger Maris, Jr. said, 'You're dad's number one fan.'

"Now I go back to Fargo every year for a charity golf tournament and auction held in Roger's name for the Hospice of the Red River Valley. One year I asked for the opportunity to address the 700 people present. I said, 'You've heard from Roger's family, Roger's friends, his teammates, but there is another side, and that is Roger's fans, and this video tells it all.'

"The lights went down and on came a 3½ minute video I had put together with a friend—pictures of Maris, of Maris and me together, with Lou Rawls singing in the background: 'Did you know that you're my hero? You are the wind beneath my wings.' It gave me the opportunity to tell everyone about Roger Maris, the man."

Roger Maris and Andy Strasberg both had high self-esteem.

How to Become an Assertive Person

Assertive behavior is the middle ground between aggressive and passive behavior. To be assertive, one must modify five facets of his behavior: eye contact, body language, voice tone and pitch, body posture, and place and timing of action.

Aggressive: Expressing your emotions openly by using threatening behavior toward a person or object, which violates another's rights.

Passive: Hiding your emotions so that others do not know how you feel; not standing up for your rights.

Assertive: Expressing your emotions honestly and standing up for your rights without hurting others.

Aggressive Behavior Description

1. Eye Contact: Constant eye contact, glaring, staring

I learn something and useful from every positive-minded person I meet.

2. Facial Expression: Frown, tight-lipped, jaw set, no smile, mouthing words, threatening
3. Body Position: Feet wide apart, standing
4. Gestures: Shaking arm, fist, or finger; waving arms threateningly
5. Personal Space: Very close to person or thing addressed
6. Voice: Harsh, threatening tone
7. Volume: Loud, or low and threatening

Understanding Aggressive Behavior

Aggressive behavior lets us express our feelings, but hurts others. It is appropriate only in life-threatening situations or contact sports like football. We act aggressively both verbally and nonverbally. Verbally, we scream. Nonverbally, we threaten others with our arms, fists, and bodies by hitting, shoving, or shaking our fists. Most importantly, aggressive behavior in inappropriate places may let us say how we feel, but it usually results in a negative consequence (being hit back, detention in school, suspension from work, etc.).

Passive Behavior Description

1. Eye Contact: Little or none, often looking down, doesn't meet others' eyes
2. Facial Expression: Little or no emotion, slight smile
3. Gestures: Arms folded limply or close to side; little or no motion with arms or hands
4. Posture: Feet together, head down, shoulders slumped, does not stand close to others
5. Voice: Soft
6. Volume: Mumbles; inaudible, soft voice

Understanding Passive Behavior

Passive people let others take advantage of them because their behavior doesn't allow them to express their feelings and

---

No man stands as tall as he who makes other people more productive.

prevents them from standing up for themselves. Nonverbal passive behaviors include looking at the floor or away from others and standing with head down and shoulders slumped. Verbal passive behavior is speaking softly, sometimes so that people can't hear. Often passive people are often ignored by others.

Assertive Behavior Description

1. Eye Contact: Intermittently looking directly at other person
2. Facial Expressions: Showing emotion, pleasant, smiling, questioning
3. Posture: Relaxed, shoulders back, head up, facing the other person, feet a comfortable distance apart
4. Gestures: Nods head, uses hands and arms to show feelings and thoughts (in a nonthreatening manner)
5. Voice: Normal tone, easily heard, polite

Understanding Assertive Behavior

Assertive behavior lets us express how we feel about something or stand up for our rights without hurting others. Assertive nonverbal behaviors include good eye contact; gesturing to emphasize what we are saying; using smiles, interested expressions, laughter, or questioning looks as facial expressions; standing with head and shoulders back and comfortably near the person to whom we are speaking. Assertive verbal behaviors include a normal speaking voice that is loud enough for others to hear. This behavior lets us say what we feel or think; but we should realize we may not always get what we want.

How to Live in the Joy of High Self-Esteem

1. See yourself as a positive, enthusiastic, growing, and achieving person with genuine self-esteem.

"I use all the brains I have, and all I can borrow."
Pres. Woodrow Wilson

2. Rid yourself of all negative emotions and learn to meet your own emotional needs.

3. Learn the values of relating to people—your children, friends, and the people you date. Trust yourself to grow.

4. Remember where you were and acknowledge where you are now. Then you have the confidence to become what you want to be. Don't consider marriage until you can give of the overflow of your wholeness.

5. Be sure you have reevaluated your values and rejected those that are unworthy of you. For example, it is more important to value people and use things than to use people and value things. You must be in a position of caring, sharing, and giving, rather than demanding.

6. You must have come through the process of being in charge of your life. No one else will or should do for you the things you can do for yourself. You are neither dependent nor independent, but interdependent.

7. It is necessary to respect the personhood of each individual. You no longer fit people into confining grooves, but realize the uniqueness of every person.

8. You no longer make snap judgments of people. You trust yourself, so you now can trust others, expect the best, and look for the good in others.

9. Now you can face and handle your own problems rather than look for a rescuer to solve problems for you. You have the well-deserved confidence that you can overcome most any adversity.

10. You are now a unique, self-celebrating person of value. You control your own mind with positive thoughts; you

"By virtue of being born to humanity, every human being has a right to the development and fulfillment of his potentialities as a human being."

Ashley Montagu

control your own emotions by relating only to those people you choose to relate to.
11. You are free to be you. Now, if the right people come into your life, you can choose to relate to them. You are on your way to a meaningful, purposeful, and fulfilling life.

Quotes

"The success in life is for a man to be ready for his opportunity when it comes."

British Prime Minister Benjamin Disraeli

"It is a funny thing about life. If you refuse to accept anything but the best, you often get it."   Somerset Maugham

"Always behave like a duck. Keep calm and unruffled on the surface but paddle like the devil underneath."

Anonymous

"The three really great things in the world are a mountain, the ocean, and an earnest man at his work. The potentialities of each are beyond human calculation."

Edward W. Bok

"Genius is one percent inspiration and ninety-nine perspiration."   Thomas Edison

"If you are a self-made man, you are working on a job that will never be finished."   Anonymous

"Far better it is to dare mighty things to win glorious triumphs, even though checkered by failure, than to take rank with those poor spirits who neither enjoy much nor suffer much, because they live in the gray twilight that knows not victory, only defeat."   Pres. Theodore Roosevelt

---

"He who is firm and resolute in will molds the world to himself."
Goethe

"Success is like a good movie: It is only exciting when you have someone to share it with."   Anonymous

"If you have built castles in the air, your work need not be lost: That is where they should be. Now put foundations under them."   Henry David Thoreau

"The world stands aside to let anyone pass who knows where he is going."   David Starr Jordan

"No man can be happy unless he feels his life is in some way important."   Bertrand Russell

"One person with a belief is equal to a force of 99 who have interests."   John Stuart Mill

"Always do right. This will gratify some people and astonish the rest."   Mark Twain

"There is no security on this earth. There is only opportunity."   Gen. Douglas MacArthur

"You cannot climb the ladder of success with your hands in your pockets."   Anonymous

"There are those who are so scrupulously afraid of doing wrong that they seldom venture to do anything."
                    Anonymous

"There are no great men, only great challenges that ordinary men are forced by circumstances to meet."
                    Adm. William F. Bull Halsey

"Our greatest joy is not in never falling, but rising every time we fail."   Confucius

"The really happy man is the one who can enjoy the scenery when he has to take a detour."   Anonymous

---

I can control the way I feel about others for I choose not to yield my good thoughts and feelings to negative and destructive thoughts and feelings.

"You can have anything out of life you want, if you help enough people get what they want."   Zig Ziglar

"We are forever on the verge of all that is great: trust in yourself, claim your share of the greatness of life: surrender yourself to the power within you: dare to become the master of your own fate."   Ralph Waldo Emerson

How to Develop Genuine Self-Esteem

1. Fact: God wants you to love yourself. Nineteen times in the Bible we are commanded to love ourselves.
2. Desire to change your life. Decide what more you want out of life and do it.
3. Put yourself first. Then out of your self, love overflows; others will benefit.
4. Perform the program of change. Write out your goals, commit yourself to them, and achieve them.
5. Get in touch with yourself, with your feelings, your mind, your will, and become a whole person.
6. Practice the policy of benefiting others. Enjoy the positive power of giving sunshine to others.
7. Enjoy meaningful work production. Give more than you expect to receive and the law of compensation will pay off for you.
8. Improve your physical health. Get in shape and stay in shape. Fatigue makes cowards of us all.
9. Improve your mental health. Enjoy spirited conversation, read challenging books, and stretch your mind.
10. Improve your social health. Give yourself the greatest gift of good friends. Enjoy theater, music, travel, nature, dining, and and other good social experiences.
11. Improve your spiritual health. Rid yourself of unhealthy guilt feelings. Learn to accept God's love.
12. Increase your pleasure activity. Decide and enjoy pleasure free of regret.

The harder I work, and the better I plan, the luckier I get.

13. Feed yourself good strokes. Learn to meet your own emotional needs.
14. Plan an achieving life. You pass through this life but once. Make it a great life. The only thing you and I can totally control are our own minds.

Self-esteem comes from
1. Meaningful work production
2. Good human relations
3. God-love, romantic love, family love, and self-love.
4. Enjoyable recreation
5. Music, worship, nature, and other values

Self-love, self-esteem, self-confidence, self-value, and self-celebration are yours. Live it up. You are of value, you are important, and you are beautiful.

Self-Esteem

1. I am the best friend to myself. I take me out whenever I feel low. I alone am responsible for my feelings and I choose to feel beautiful.
2. I am a unique, never-to-be-repeated miracle of God. Therefore, today, and every day, I celebrate myself.
3. I live in the principle of unlimitedness. Abundance is mine for love, peace, joy, happiness, energy, health, and wealth know no boundaries.
4. I am open, receptive, responsive and obedient to life, love, joy, peace, energy, wealth, health, wisdom, and the beauty of wholeness.
5. A new friend is a beautiful gift I give myself.
6. No one can make me stoop so low as to hate him.
7. I draw people to me by the power of my love for them.

"Love cures people. Both the ones who give it,
and the ones who receive it."
Dr. Karl Menninger

8. I will not be an emotional cripple controlled by negative attitudes.
9. I relate to positive-minded people and choose not to expose my sensitive emotions to negative-minded people, for such thoughts are destructive.
10. I dwell on beautiful, powerful thoughts of self-affirmation.
11. My personality is the outward expression of the inward person. I want that person to be fulfilling and whole, so I will love myself and be loved by others.
12. The happiest people are those with experience in helping others.
13. I will remember that the deepest urge in human nature is the desire to be important, and I will sincerely and honestly seek to make every person I meet feel important.
14. I can develop the skill of getting along with people.
15. I can cure many of my ills by helping friends cure theirs.
16. I can control the way I feel about others, because I choose not to yield my good thoughts and feelings for negative and destructive thoughts and feelings.
17. I believe in the redeeming power of God's love.
18. "For as he thinketh in his heart, so is he. . . ." (Prov. 23:7).
19. God is my instant, constant, abundant source of energy, love, and peace.
20. "And all things, whatsoever ye shall ask in prayer, believing, ye shall receive." (Matt. 21:22).
21. The love of God lives in me, the peace of God lives as me, the power of God flows through me; wherever I am God is, and all is well.
22. I have faith in the power of the human body to heal through nutrition.

Not failure, but low aim, is the real crime in life.

23. From my healthy body and my healthy thoughts, I live
     an abundant life.

Conclusion

Regardless of what you have suffered from the past of poor self-esteem, only you can change these feelings. Determine your
script, erase the bad feelings, and replace them with the
positive self-affirmations to become the person God intended you to be. Only when you have bombarded your
subconscious mind with more positive self-talk than the total of negative self-talk will you become a positive person.

Realize you and you alone must be responsible for who you are.
Become your own self-nurturing parent.

This is a lifelong journey toward wholeness and happiness. You
are not alone. There are many others available to help you.
Your public library is full of self-help books.

A friend is someone who loves and cares.

CHAPTER 9

Self-Esteem in Relationships: How to Enjoy Real Love

In order to appreciate and share love as an adult, children must grow through the following steps and have the various needs met, as originally theorized by psychologist Abraham Maslow:

1. Physical Needs—food, lodging, and a sense that physical needs will be adequately provided for.
2. Safety Needs—freedom from fear, worry, abuse, and hostility, so that one feels safe and secure.
3. Social Needs—a warm feeling and satisfaction of belonging to parents, other family members, peer groups, church, school, and God.
4. Love Needs—unquestioned acceptance of God's love, parents' love, family love, friends' love, and self-love.
5. Self-Actualization—exciting growth toward fullness, wholeness, and completeness; a strong assurance that one can achieve any goal desired.
6. Peak-Experiencing—beautiful mental and emotional overflowing feelings of God's blessing, goal-seeking, strong assurance of direction, warm satisfaction, and self-celebration. Directly proportionate to this achievement is the adult able to give and receive real love.

One is growing in real love when one is more dedicated to the satisfaction, security, growth, happiness, and self-esteem of the one loved than for one's self.

Love is not an emotion. Emotions such as passion, greed, jealousy, ambition, strife, etc. are uncontrolled feelings that fluctuate like a yo-yo.

Love is an activity. It is growing in, not "falling in." Love is the activity of giving, sharing, communicating, experiencing, and becoming.

Real love has feelings as a result of this activity—overflowing, alive, joyful, and exciting feelings built on the firm foundation of assured and proven conduct instead of the insecurity of an uncontrolled passion.

Love is a decision. It is a commitment to love based on common values and compatibility in spiritual, mental, financial, character, family, vocation, happiness, and openness beliefs.

Love is unconditional. You do not turn off your love when another irritates you. You love without reservation. You like or dislike conduct.

Love is forever. Without this intent, you do not give love your best.

Love is a decision to grow, to love, to be fulfilled, and to achieve happiness.

Love affirms, not possesses. Love doesn't smother, but sets free. If you love someone, set him free. If he comes back to you, he is yours forever. If he doesn't, he never was yours in the first place.

How to Give Real Love Worksheet

On a scale of one to ten, rate yourself on these steps of self-actualization:

_____ 1. *Physical Needs.* I am free of concern for my physical needs such as food, lodging and financial pressure.

---

*Today and every day, I look for people who want
to share my journey toward greatness.*

___ 2. *Safety Needs.* I feel safe where I live and feel secure from fear, worry, hostility, and negative emotions.

___ 3. *Social Needs.* I have a strong feeling of belonging to my parents, family, church, friends, and to God.

___ 4. *Love Needs.* I really love myself and am able to give and receive love from God, parents, other relatives, friends of the same sex, and friends of the opposite sex.

___ 5. *Self-Actualization.* I enjoy my journey toward fullness, wholeness, completeness, and achievement.

___ 6. Peak-Experiencing. On occasion, I experience a peak of wonderful feelings of emotional overflowing.

___ 7. Now I am able to give security, satisfaction, self-esteem, and happiness to the one I love.

___ 8. I have made a decision of emotions, mind, and the will to commit my love. I give this wonderful gift as the highest expression of my personhood.

___ 9. I give my love unconditionally, as I appreciate and chose my mate for her/his values and character.

___ 10. I commit my love forever. I hold no reservation, because I intend this experience to last a lifetime.

___ 11. I am open to growth and communication in every area with my intended.

___ 12. My love empowers my mate to love her/himself.

___ 13. I affirm my mate and will not possess her/him.

___ Total

---

*"Happiness is a perfume that you cannot pour on
someone else without getting a few drops on yourself."*
Ralph Waldo Emerson

Scoring

100—130   You are a strong, emotionally mature, actual-izing person able to give genuine, real love.

80—99   You are growing toward self-acceptance and desire an achieving life.

60—79   You have areas in your life that need facing so you can proceed on your journey toward full-ness.

40—59   Work through your emotions in order to ac-cept yourself. Only then will you be able to give love to another.

Getting to Know Yourself

I like myself better when _____

_____

I feel bad when _____

_____

I am at my best when _____

_____

I feel good when _____

_____

My greatest asset is _____

My most important need is _____

My greatest accomplishment is _____

_____

_____

*"You make more friends in two months by becoming
interested in other people than you can in two years
by trying to get other people interested in you."*
Dale Carnegie

My intellectual hero is _____

My spiritual hero is _____

My political hero is _____

If I could change one thing in my life _____

_____

The best time of my life was _____

_____

The worst time of my life was _____

_____

Check up on your relationships. Separately, sit down and grade your mate (or a friend) on a scale of 1-10 on each of these areas:

1. Shared goals   ____

2. Values   ____

3. Communication   ____

4. Spiritual unity   ____

5. Social satisfaction   ____

6. Touching, affection   ____

7. Positive method of conflict   ____

8. Male/female identity   ____

9. Sexual fulfillment   ____

10. Compatibility with friends   ____

11. Food and drink experiences   ____

12. Individual growth   ____

It pays to share. The more you pass on to others, the more you get to have for yourself.

13. Decision making   ___

14. Fun and play time   ___

15. Intimate talk time   ___

16. Freedom and independence   ___

17. Parenting   ___

18. Recreation fulfillment   ___

19. Vacation and travel   ___

20. Financial agreement   ___

                              Total   ___

Scoring

Less than 100	poor relationship
101—125	fair relationship
176—200	great relationship

Any area where the rating was less than 5 is the area you need to work on. Here is where you have problems. Talk this over with your mate (or friend). Encourage him (or her) to communicate openly. Work on your relationship.

Living the Spirit of Cooperation

Plentifulness. With openness, discussion, good communication, and fulfilling mutual experiences, each person can have all the strokes, values, joys, achievements, and self-celebration he or she may desire. The more love you share, the more you have. There is no limitedness in love.

Equal Partners. Each verbalizes what he/she wants, can give and contract for strokes, financial security, work responsibility, love-sharing, and every mutual experience.

What makes men great is their ability to decide what is important, and to then focus their attention to it.

Lovingly, call the other on power plays. Since there can be no losers in a cooperation, and no tyranny, you openly and lovingly call the other's hand when winner-versus-loser power plays are consciously or subconsciously expressed. Only then can preconceived roles be discontinued.

Ask for what you want 100 percent of the time. No one can meet your needs if you yourself don't know what they are. Hold no secrets from the other, but let it all hang out. With each request, there may be a compromise response. Then contract for what you want.

Don't rescue, but help when agreed upon. To rescue means there must be a victim. The rescuer says, "I know what you need and I'll give it to you whether or not you want it." The helper says, "I can give you 'warm fuzzies' or emotional affirmations if you want me to."

The rules:

You don't help unless you contract to do so.
Your mate is able to help himself/herself.
You help your mate to achieve fullness.
You do no more than fifty percent of the process.
Do only what you want to do.

These principles also should apply to parent-child, boss-employee, and friend-friend relationships.

Creating Ecstasy in Your Relationships

1. Are you willing for your relationship to work?
2. Do you really want satisfaction in your relationships?
3. Do you desire completion in your relationships?
4. Do you strongly desire aliveness and vitality in your relationships?
5. Do you want certainty and constancy in your relationships?

The only way to have a friend is to be one.

6. Do you give completeness and commitment in your relationships?
7. Do you know what you want in your relationships (family, friends, romance)?
8. Can you pinpoint what has happened to end other relationships?
9. Do you remain friendly with others when the relationship is over?
10. Can you look back and appreciate what you learned and experienced in other relationships?
11. Can you honestly evaluate how you contributed to the failure of former relationships?
12. How much of the failure of former relationships was due to relating to the wrong person for you?
13. Do you need to be more careful in choosing your relationships?
14. Have you tended to hold back and not give your best effort in a relationship?
15. Do you clearly know what you want in a relationship?
16. Do you openly and honestly tell the other person what you want?
17. Do you tend to get too involved too soon in a romantic relationship?
18. Are you looking for someone to meet your needs in a romantic relationship?
19. Do you know how to heal a troubled relationship?
20. How would you like to have a recreational relationship?
21. Are you willing to take the time to let the relationship develop naturally?
22. Do you tend to become too possessive in a relationship?

"You can cure your ills by helping a friend cure his."
Dale Carnegie

23. Do you know how to give "space" in a relationship?
24. Are you capable of giving more to a relationship than you take from it?
25. Who is the source of love in a relationship?
26. In a relationship of two others close to you, who is the source of love?
27. Who do you need in order to experience love?
28. If love is scarce in your relationship, who isn't creating love?
29. Have you learned how to love a person into loving you?
30. From whom do we draw out love?
31. Do you know how to create love and how to do it consistently?

Ecstasy. A state of feeling of overpowering joy.

Relationship. Understanding and awareness of another person's way of being. Living as the other person. Thinking and acting as the other person.

Involvement. Making life intricate, full of puzzles, full of elaborate detail, entangled, endangered, and difficult to catch so that escape is nearly impossible.

Completeness. To make whole, full, perfect; inclusion of all that is needed for wholeness. No need for something else, no sense of being difficult. No sense it could be better, no sense of inadequacy. Perfect and accepted as is.

Create. To cause to come into existence, to make, to originate, to bring about, to cause, to give rise to.

Space. The boundless expanse within which all things are contained, room for self, personhood, soul, being, an interval of time.

"This is the true joy in life: that being used for a purpose recognized by yourself as a mighty one, being a force of nature, rather than a feverish, selfish little clod

---

My personality is the outward expression of the inward person and I want that person to be fulfilling and whole so I will love myself and be loved by others.

of ailments and grievances, complaining that the world will not devote itself to making me happy. . . . Life is no brief candle to me, but a sort of splendid torch which I've got a hold of for the moment and I want to make it burn as brightly as possible before handing it on to future generations."

George Bernard Shaw

We Relate to People We Admire and Respect

Sydney Smith said, "Life is to be fortified by many friendships. To love and be loved, is the greatest happiness of existence." Quit trying to get along with people you don't admire and respect. You have a relationship problem with these people. Cultivate the relationship with time, energy, activity, concern, and love. For this is the only basis of a real relationship.

Look back on failed relationships, marriages, courtships, etc. Wasn't this the reason for its dissolution?

What are the values that you admire and respect? List as many as you can.

1. _____   4. _____

2. _____   5. _____

3. _____   6. _____

Now, look back on experiences that didn't work out—a parent, brother or sister, mate or friend. Do you see why? Don't feel guilty. You have a right to be you and have your own values. Anyone who doesn't measure up to them isn't to be blamed. That's the way life works.

Draw people to you by the power of your love for them.

Creating Space

Rainer Maria Rilke said, "Love consists in this, that two solitudes protect and touch and greet each other."

Space is personhood—the sacredness of the human soul; the preciousness of the individual personality; the priceless dignity of an eternal person. No one has the right to injure, hurt, hinder, harass, limit, embarrass, or damage someone's personhood.

Think back and recall some times when you were so damaged. List them:

1. _____ 3. _____

2. _____ 4. _____

Think back and recall some ways you have violated the personhood of another.

1. _____ 3. _____

2. _____ 4. _____

Space is privacy. In what ways has your privacy been denied? In what ways have you violated the privacy of another person?

1. _____ 3. _____

2. _____ 4. _____

Space is values. List some of your values others have violated:

1. _____ 3. _____

2. _____ 4. _____

*"I have found that if I have faith in myself and
in the idea I am tinkering with, I usually win out."*
Charles F. Kettering

Space is time. How do you feel others are violating your time?

1. _____   3. _____

2. _____   4. _____

Living the "No Wrong" Life

Eleanor Roosevelt said, "No one can make you feel inferior without your consent." You and I do not have the right to make others feel that they are wrong. We are not God. They do not have to answer to us. And you violate any opportunity to bring about change or to influence other people when you make them feel wrong. List some ways others have made you feel wrong:

1. _____   3. _____

2. _____   4. _____

Now list some ways you have unwittingly made another person feel wrong.

1. _____   3. _____

2. _____   4. _____

We are carrying on our backs a load of garbage or a load of gold. Don't dump garbage on others. Instead, shower them with gold dust, or even a nugget or two.

Goal-Seeking

Anyone can set a goal. The realization of goals is dependent on two other factors: a change of attitude in that you act as if your goal is now yours, and conduct of activity

"Every great and commanding moment in the annals of the world is the triumph of some enthusiasm."
Ralph Waldo Emerson

that assures the achievement of your goal. Nothing becomes dynamic until it becomes specific. Write out your goals as clearly and concisely as possible. Let this stimulate you:

What problems in the relationship do you want resolved?

_____

What are you now doing in the relationship that you want to stop doing?

_____

_____

What are you not doing in the relationship that you want to start doing?

_____

_____

What fantasy or desire do you want fulfilled?

_____

_____

What do you feel needs to be done to make the relationship more complete?

_____

_____

What travels, possessions, or experiences do you want to experience in the relationship?

_____

_____

Build a reservoir of good will by placing the interest of others above your own.

Growing the Relationship

Walter Winchell said, "A friend is one who walks in when others walk out."

Put energy into it. Assign priority to it. Friendship is as important as eating, sleeping, and working. Satisfaction is followed by dissatisfaction.

The strongest of life's desires is to feel important. With this is the desire to reveal our innermost self. With your trusted friend, really open up as to who you are, what you want, and what you want to become.

Enjoy touching. "There is one temple in the universe— the human body. We touch heaven when we touch the human body." (Thomas Carlyle) More than a million sensory fibers flow from the skin through the spinal cord to the brain. Our skin is the most powerful organ in the body. Reveal your love, your warmth, and your wholeness by touching.

Constantly affirm. Never let the other person doubt your support, love, concern, assurance, and availability. Spoken and written words are so important. Pablo Casals said, "As long as one can admire and love, then one is young forever."

Loyalty. Nothing will ever be allowed to sever or weaken the relationship. This loyalty can bring back from disaster a person to renewed ecstasy.

Creating ecstasy. There are two states of being:

1. Planned achievement. This comes as the result of a process. Maslow's six steps to self-actualization is an example. Learning is a process.

2. Instant achievement. This is the statement of a desired truth. The human mind, at least the subconscious part, is very vague. The conscious mind gives clear-cut commands and the subconscious mind instantly obeys. You can create a miracle by the decision to do so.

"Love and you shall be loved."
Ralph Waldo Emerson

There is a four-thought pattern toward this accomplishment:

1. *Desire.* Strong enough to be willing to change.
2. *Expectancy.* By faith accepting it as truth.
3. *Behaving as fact.* From this moment on, it is a fact and nothing will change it.
4. *Reinforcement.* With affirmations, attitude control, and conduct response, you can continue to reinforce the decision. You must never look back.

Whatever you tell yourself and believe, it is then truth for you and you behave accordingly. *You have now created ecstasy. You live the truth of overpowering joy.*

How to Communicate with Your Mate

1. What is the funniest thing that ever happened to you?
2. Where did you spend the most delicious weekend of your life?
3. What is your favorite movie? Favorite book? Favorite food? Favorite music?
4. Who was your hero as a child? As an adult?
5. On a scale of one to ten, rate yourself as a loving, caring person.
6. Rate yourself as to your openness, your honesty, and your friendliness.
7. Rate yourself as to your being fun to be with.
8. Rate yourself as to your sensuousness. Rate your ambition. Rate your happiness.
9. If you had but one year to live, what would you do?
10. If you had one year to live, *and money were no object,* what would you do?
11. What member of your family are you closest to? Who is your closest friend?
12. If you had an overwhelming problem, to whom would you go?

To be a free person is life's greatest achievement.

13. What parent are you closest to? What child? What brother or sister?

14. Who is your best friend of the same sex? Nonromantic friend of opposite sex?

15. Who is your most spiritual friend? Most emotionally mature friend?

16. What do you want most in a friend? In a mate?

17. Name an activity you hate to do. Name an activity your mate hates to do.

18. If you had but one word to describe yourself, what would it be?

19. If you had but one word to describe your mate, what would it be?

20. What do you like most about your mate?

21. What do you like least about your mate?

22. What is the best value you add to your mate's life?

23. What is the best value your mate adds to your life?

24. What is the greatest thing you have received from this relationship?

25. What do you want most from this relationship?

26. What have you learned from this relationship?

27. What would you like to contribute most to this relationship?

28. What in life is the most important to you? To your mate?

29. What is the most important for you and your mate to share?

30. What would you like to change in the way your mate acts toward you?

31. What should you change in the way you act toward your mate?

32. Close your eyes. What was the happiest expression ever on your mate's face?

I choose not to be an emotional cripple controlled by the negative attitudes of others.

33. What was the most pained expression you have ever seen on your mate's face?
34. What do you feel when your mate looks lovingly at you?
35. What do you feel when your mate lovingly touches you?
36. What do you feel when your mate says he/she loves you?
37. Is there anything you would like your mate to tell you that he/she hasn't?
38. Is there anything you would like to tell your mate that you haven't?
39. How do you feel when you are alone and you think about your mate?
40. Does your mate ever make you feel sad? Was it your activity that caused it?
41. Do you ever make your mate feel sad? Why? By accident or with intent?
42. What first attracted you to your mate? What continues to attract you?
43. If you could go anywhere in the world with your mate, where would it be?
44. Do you think you spend too much time with your mate? Too little time?
45. What physical feature of your mate do you like the most?
46. What physical feature of your mate do you like the least?
47. What emotional feature of your mate do you like the most?
48. What emotional feature of your mate do you like the least?
49. What spiritual feature of your mate do you like the most?

God will not bestow blessings on you if there is no
room in your heart to receive them.

50. What spiritual feature of your mate do you like the least?
51. What habit of your mate do you like the least?
52. When you are away from your mate, what do you miss the most?
53. What do you need most from your mate? What does your mate need most from you?
54. What do you need to contribute most to your mate?
55. What do you want your mate to contribute most to you?
56. What do you lack most that your mate has not fulfilled?
57. What are you most emotional about?
58. When are you most in tune with God?
59. Do you ever pretend to be something you are not? Does your mate?
60. Do you ever dream about your mate?
61. Do you ever try to control or manipulate your mate? Does your mate ever try to control or manipulate you?
62. Do you ever feel smothered in this relationship? Do you ever smother?
63. When he/she came into your life, were you a happy person?
64. Are you a much happier person now? Are you more in touch with yourself now?
65. Have you grown spiritually since you have been in this relationship?
66. Have you grown mentally since you have been in this relationship? Emotionally?
67. What do you think you mean to your mate? What does your mate mean to you?
68. When was the closest you have ever felt with your mate?
69. What does your mate say that makes you feel good?

"Children who are not loved in their very beingness do not know how to love themselves. As adults, they learn to nourish, to mother their lost child."

Marion Woodman

70. What do you say that makes your mate feel good?
71. When do you enjoy your mate the most, when alone or in a group?
72. What is the greatest experience you and your mate have enjoyed?
73. You were happiest when _____
74. What is the most important wish you have for this relationship?
75. Are you willing to continue to open up and share what you feel with your mate?

Lee Iocacca is one of the most achieving people in America. He performed a miracle at Chrysler Corporation. In his book, *Talking Straight*, he describes his relationship with his family. Here are some of the highlights:

He never let his money or fame go to his head. His daughter, Lia, was asked one day in kindergarten what her father did. She answered, "I'm not sure. I think he washes cars."

He never sat and lectured the kids by saying, "Here's the way I want you to grow up." He gave them simple guidelines: that they come talk to him whenever there was a problem, not to keep it inside; never lie; never get into debt; if they ever borrowed from a friend, never forget to repay the debt; never make a promise they couldn't keep. He said, "If the kids did not make super grades, I didn't go crazy about it." He kept after them if they did below average in their classes, but if they kept with the work and kept their grades up, he was satisfied.

He placed his family first on his schedule. He spent every weekend with his family, every vacation. "Kathi was on the swim team for seven years and I never missed a meet. . . . I was afraid that if I missed one, Kathi might finish first or

---

"If we can stop one heart from breaking, we shall not live in vain.
If we can ease one life from aching, or cool one pain, or help one
feinting robin into its nest again, we shall not live in vain."
Emily Dickinson

finish last, and I would hear about it second hand and not be there to congratulate—or console her."

He tells how his daughter Lia, when she was six, had just gotten into the Potawatami Tribe at Brownie Camp. She had wanted to join the "Nava-Joes," but didn't make it. He recalls that they were both excited, regardless. "Funny thing, I missed an important meeting that day, but for the life of me, I have no recollection of what it was."

He showed love to his family. "I've always been affectionate with my kids. . . . [they] were always what mattered most . . . I love them" (*Talking Straight*, 288-89).

That is high self-esteem. Lee loved them out of the overflow of his life. If one of the busiest men in America can schedule the time to go to swim meets and plays with his children, so can you. Don't sacrifice your family on the altar of commerce.

How to Build a Better Marriage

1. Enjoy effective communication.

Cliche. This is as far as communication goes for some. Move on.

Activity. Still not enough. Sure, discuss what you both have done that day, but life is more than activity.

Attitudes and opinions. Find out how the other feels and thinks.

At the gut level. Never pass judgment on the other. Withhold moral opinions. Don't blame. Emotions must be integrated into intellect and conduct. And emotions must be reported at the time.

Peak-blending relationship. You think, feel, and act as one.

2. Develop individual self-esteem.

"Every part of your body responds to your emotions."
Robert E. Decker

He develops self-esteem in his profession, and/or her profession, family, romance, and recreation.

She develops self-esteem in her profession, and/or his profession, family, romance, and recreation.

Each encourages the other's independence, creativity, self-esteem, financial security, cultural, and aesthetic interest.

Self-esteem overflow radiates to others.

3. Participate in an equal partnership.
Openness in feelings
Nonpossessiveness
Partnership in home responsibility
Respect for privacy and individuality
Freedom to grow and encouragement of the other to grow
Annual contract of intent, not control

4. Become the ideal loving mate.
Assertive and self-confident
Rational and emotional balance and openness
Capacity and practice of sharing deepest feelings
Sincere empathy for the other's happiness
Well-defined plan for growth
Creative leisure sharing experiences
Tender, warm and achieving sensuality

Quotes on Love

"To love one who loves you, to admire one who admires you, in a word: to be the idol of one's idol is exceeding the limit of human joy: it is stealing fire from heaven."

Madame de Girardin

"Mature love is union under the condition of preserving one's integrity, one's individuality. In love, the paradox

---

You must take responsibility for your own development.

occurs that two beings become one and yet remain two."
Erich Fromm

"Love casts our fear; but, conversely, fear casts out love."
Aldous Huxley

Loneliness is the pain a person who doesn't love himself suffers. Solitude is the joy a person who loves himself experiences.

"To love is to stop comparing."   Anonymous

"The risks of love are higher than most investments. The rewards are greater than winning a sweepstakes."
Anonymous

"Forgiveness is the fragrance the violet sheds on the heel that has crushed it."   Anonymous

"Jealousy is a way of getting rid of everything you are afraid of losing."   Anonymous

"The worst sin towards our fellow creatures is not to hate them; but to be indifferent to them; that's the essence of inhumanity."   George Bernard Shaw

"It is not fair to ask of others what you are not willing to do yourself."   Eleanor Roosevelt

"Loneliness is never more cruel than when it is felt in close propinquity with someone who has ceased to communicate."   Germaine Greer

"The great secret of a successful marriage is to treat all disasters as incidents and none of the incidents as disasters."
Harold Nicolson

"True friendship comes when silence between two people is comfortable."   Dave Gentry

---

I'm Alive. . . . I'm Alert. . . . I'm Excited.

"Shared joys make a friend, not shared sufferings."

Nietzsche

"Those who love deeply never grow old. They may die of old age, but they die young." Anonymous

"The only way to have a friend is to be one."

Ralph Waldo Emerson

"There is a destiny that makes us brothers, none goes his way alone. All that we send into the lives of others comes back into our own." Edwin Markham

"The greatest discovery of my generation is that human beings can alter their lives by altering their attitudes or mine."

S. M. James

"Just remember that what you are going to be tomorrow you are becoming today." Anonymous

"Behavior is a mirror in which everyone shows his image."

Goethe

"The outward behavior of a man is at once the sign and proof of the inner self." Mahatma Gandhi

"You had better live your best, think your best and do your best today—for today will soon be tomorrow and tomorrow will soon be forever." Goethe

"The best things in life are never rationed. Friendship, love, loyalty do not require coupons." G. T. Hewill

"The doors we open and close each day decide the lives we live." Flora Whitmore

"I have yet to find the man, however exalted his station, who did not do better work and put forth greater effort under a spirit of approval, than under a spirit of criticism."

Charles Schwab

"No one can make you feel inferior without your consent."
Eleanor Roosevelt

"Our doubts are traitors and make us lose the good we oft might win by fearing to attempt."   Shakespeare

"A man is no greater than his dream, his ideal, his hope, and his plan. Man dreams the dream—and, fulfilling it, it's the dream that makes the man."   Anonymous

"If you would love me you must be on higher ground."
                    Ralph Waldo Emerson

"We may elevate ourselves, but we should never reach so high that we would ever forget those who helped us get there."   Will Rogers

"No man is free who cannot command himself."
                    Pythagoras

"In life we get what we order."   Anonymous

"Kindness is the golden chain by which society is bound to-gether."   Goethe

"To be what we are, and to become what we are capable of becoming, is the only end of life."   Spinoza

"We have committed the golden rule to memory, let us now commit it to our lives."   Edwin Markham

"Our life is what our thoughts make it."
                    Marcus Aurelius

"If we take people as we find them, we may make them worse; but if we treat them as though they are what they should be, we help them to become what they are capable of becoming."   Goethe

Conclusion

Dr. Karl Mennenger said, "The purpose of life is to delete the misery of people."
We become what the people with whom we surround ourselves are.

Our life is what our thoughts make us.

Commit yourself to giving happiness and high self-esteem to your mate, and especially to your children.

Invest time and energy in joyful daily family experiences. Sigmund Freud said, "The three most important factors in life are (1) the quality of marital and sexual relationships, (2) meaningful occupation, and (3) the quality of friends and social life."

You deserve valued and loving feedback from your family. You will receive from them only a part of what you give to them. If you want love, you must give love.

"Self-confidence is the first requisite to great undertakings."
Dale Carnegie

CHAPTER 10

Controlling Your Conduct

To control your conduct, you must have positive self-expectancy. Here's how:

Begin the day with positive self-affirmations. Take charge of your mind. The only thing in the world you can totally control is your own mind.

Invest time in positive relationships. A good friend is the best gift you give yourself.

Turn every problem into an opportunity. Ask yourself, "In what way can we . . . ?"

Control your stress. Learn to relax and enjoy the luxury of leisure.

Improve your health with powerful exercise.

Use only positive statements with others. Accentuate your strengths.

Invest valuable time in improved family relationships.

Look for and expect the best in others. Challenge others to achieve their best.

Choose to associate with positive-minded people. We become whatever the crowd we run with is.

Expect each day to be a happy experience. Say to yourself:

> I'm going to be happy today,
> Though the skies may be cloudy and gray;
> No matter what may come my way,
> I'm going to be happy today.

The Power of Mind

Reader's Digest told the story of a high school class that proved the power of the mind. People with equal ability were divided into three groups. Group I was told not to practice shooting free throws for a month. Group II practiced shooting 100 free throws each day for a month. Group III was told to imagine they were shooting 100 free throws each day for a month.

Group I, with no practice for a month, slipped from a 39% to a 37% free-throw average.

Group II, who practiced in the gym, increased from a 39% to a 41% free-throw average.

Group III, who practiced in their imaginations, went from a 39% to a 42.5% free-throw average.

On January 16, 1973, I attended the Super Bowl in the Los Angeles Coliseum when the Miami Dolphins completed their perfect 17-0 season with a win over the Washington Redskins, 14-7.

During the half, Andy Williams was singing in the field with the entire playing field covered by bands, cheerleaders, and others. Foster Brooks, the comedian, was seated just behind me. While Andy was singing, Foster stood up and called out to two guys some ten rows ahead of us who had just thrown a couple of oranges on the field, one hitting a cheerleader in the back. Foster said, "You two guys throwing oranges, my friends and I are very disappointed in you, aren't we, friends?" And he turned to all the fans around us and said, "Nod your heads, friends, if you are disappointed in these two guys throwing oranges." And we all nodded. Then Foster said, "I want you two guys—Hey! Look here, you two guys. I and all my friends want you to

"If one man can enhance his position in life by
self-proclamation, then why not?"

Joe Theismann

promise us you won't throw any more oranges. Do you agree? Nod your heads." And they did.

When he sat down, I told Foster, "That was the best use of crowd psychology I have ever seen."

He answered, "I've worked clubs for many years. You have to learn how to handle the guy who is drunk and wants to take over the act. You use the crowd against him. You make him the victim and you become the hero. The crowd will always side with the innocent party."

We learn to take charge of our conduct by controlling our minds. It's not easy, but anything that's as important as handling our emotions is worth the effort.

Suggestions for Emotional Well-Being

1. Make an effort to love yourself as well as everyone else.
2. Make an effort to do things that provide you with a sense of fulfillment, joy, and purpose.
3. You can choose to nourish, support, and encourage yourself.
4. Be sure to express all of your feelings, because once they are out, they lose their power to control you, to tie you up in knots.
5. You can choose to record your feelings and dreams in a daily journal.
6. If you hold pictures in your mind of what you truly want in life, you have an idea of what your goals are and how to achieve them.
7. View everything in your life, every circumstance, as an opportunity for growth and learning.
8. You can join a support group of people with similar problems and interests; this may enable you to recognize other ways to deal with things. And the support group can show you that you're never alone in your problems.

The difference between what I am and what I become is what I do.

The above list is adapted from Bernie Siegel's *Love, Medicine and Miracles*, published in New York by HarperCollins in 1986.

Finding and Meeting the Needs of Others

Basic needs:

1. To give love out of the wholeness of self-love and then to love others
2. Food, home, and safety from harm
3. A sense of self-worth
4. Financial security
5. Living a life that is needed by others and useful to others
6. Assurance of life after death
7. Fellowship with family and friends
8. Reasonable good health and activity that produces happiness
9. Belonging, enjoying meaningful fellowship with others, and being in harmony with God
10. A life that works

"There is no value judgment more important to man than the estimate he passes on himself."

Nathaniel Branden

Stanley Coopersmith, author of *Antecedents of Self-Esteem*, defines self-esteem as *the evaluation which the individual makes and customarily maintains with regard to himself; it expresses an attitude of approval or disapproval and indicates the extent to which the individual believes himself to be capable, significant, successful, and worthy.* Self-esteem is learned, not genetically acquired.

Experienced teachers have come to know, and research

I reveal the way I feel by the things I think and do.
When I change the things I think and do, I change my feelings, too.

supports, Norman Vincent Peale's observation: "There is a deep tendency in human nature to become precisely what we imagine or picture ourselves to be. We ourselves determine either self-limitation or unlimited growth potential."

A negative thinker engages in a self-destructive process, activating the world around him by sending out negative thoughts and drawing negative thoughts back to himself. The positive thinker constantly sends out positive messages that activate the world around him positively, thus drawing to himself positive results.

Four Sources of High Self-Esteem

1. Amount of respectful, accepting and concerned treatment the individual receives from the significant others in his life. We value ourselves as we are valued.
2. Successes and the status and position we hold in the world. Successes bring recognition and are thereby related to our status. Successes are the building blocks of self-esteem.
3. Living up to aspirations that the individual regards as personally significant.
4. Responding to devaluation. Demeaning actions by others (assuming that these actions do not include those by parents and teachers) is a fact of life. The ability to cope successfully with these put-downs is the key to healthy self-esteem.

Additional Sources of Self-Esteem

Power. The ability to influence and control others and the environment in which we live.

Importance. The acceptance, attention, and affection of others. The more frequent and the more varied the sources

"The truest wisdom, in general, is a resolute determination."
Napoleon

of appreciation and approval, the more positive will be the self-approval and self-esteem.

Competence. Successful performance in meeting the demands for achievement. In whatever area it may be, competence, resulting in the recognition and approval of others, is very important in developing self-esteem.

Value. Adherence to a code of moral, ethical, and religious principles. Our moral beliefs are a vital part of the framework that makes us responsible people. When our conduct is in agreement with our moral beliefs, we feel good within ourselves. When we violate our moral beliefs, we feel rotten, especially when we have hurt or damaged another person.

What we put back into our world should be more than what we have taken out as a reasonable payment for our right to live in this world. When we influence other people for their good, when our achievement results in approval and appreciation of others, when our effectiveness in life measures up to our own desire for excellence, when our values benefit mankind and leave a better place for our having been here, we will enjoy high self-esteem.

The key to controlling your conduct is to never take the bait others offer you. If you yield to their emotions, they have taken control of your life. You are out of control. Remember, your emotions are in your control.

Some years ago, I was driving from Atlanta, Georgia, to South Florida. I stopped in Orlando, late at night, to sleep. I called a friend of mine, Jim, and suggested we meet for breakfast the next morning.

We met in the motel lobby at 7 A.M. and waited for the dining room to open. The waitresses were seated, having their

---

"Jesus said unto him, 'If thou canst believe, all things are possible to him that believeth.' "
Mark 9:23

coffee, but had not opened the room for guests. At 7:20 I asked if we could come in and have coffee.

One of the waitresses answered in a gruff voice, "Sit anywhere you want to; I don't care." After Jim and I had seated ourselves, she came over and said, "Well, what do you birds want?"

I greeted her with a smile, called her Rosa from the name tag on her dress and said, "I'd like a cup of coffee, bacon, scrambled eggs, orange juice, and a glass of water." Jim gave his order, and with a scowl, Rosa left.

Jim said, "We don't have to take this. Let's go somewhere else to eat."

I replied, "Jim, how many people are you going to see today?"

He replied, "Maybe thirty."

I said, "And I will see about thirty also. If we let her make us mad, then you and I will emotionally contaminate sixty people today. That sixty will contaminate sixty each tomorrow for a total of 360, that group will do the same the next day, by the end of the week, the entire state of Florida will be at each other's throats. Let's see if we can change Rosa."

When Rosa returned with our coffee, I said to her, "Rosa, I was in a restaurant the other day and I said to the waitress, 'Do you serve crabs?' She said, '"Sit down, we'll serve anybody."'"

Rosa smiled. The next time she came with our water, I said, "Rosa, I asked that waitress for a piece of raisin pie. She shook her head and said, 'That isn't raisin, that's coconut.'" Rosa really laughed.

When she came to bring us a coffee refill, I said, "Rosa, the epitaph of the waitress is, 'The Lord finally caught her eye.'" Rosa roared.

When she brought us our checks, she asked, "Are you guys coming back for lunch today?"

In life, we get what we order.

Jim said, "No." I promised to come back the first time I was back in Orlando.

Then Rosa said, "Last night I had the worst night of my life. If I had had a pistol, I would have killed myself. I came to work today feeling the worst of my life. With your jokes and interest in me, I can make it. Thank you." Tears cascaded down her cheeks.

By controlling our emotions and conduct, we were able to turn Rosa around.

By living the following affirmations, you too can take charge of your emotions and conduct. Repeat the affirmation of the day over and over and seek to live the truth expressed.

Affirmations for the Month

1. TODAY, I , _____ , was created with an unlimited capacity for love, joy, and fulfillment.
2. TODAY, I , _____ , accept the truth of this affirmation and live for growth and wholeness.
3. TODAY, I , _____ , release and remove all barriers of fear so I can receive all blessings.
4. TODAY, I , _____ , live in the positive truths of love, joy, peace, serenity, and prosperity.
5. TODAY, I , _____ , receive and give self-confidence, self-love, and self-celebration.
6. TODAY, I , _____ , reward myself for every accomplishment and every achievement.
7. TODAY, I , _____ , am learning to love myself more in every way as a gift of God's love.
8. TODAY, I , _____ , respect my own uniqueness, individuality, and personhood.
9. TODAY, I , _____ , meet my own emotional needs because I will not be dependent on anyone else.

I choose not to be an emotional cripple, controlled by
the negative attitudes of others.

10. TODAY, I , _____ , no longer am dependent on others to affirm me, because I do that myself.

11. TODAY, I , _____ , like, value, and please myself, and renounce forever self-criticism.

12. TODAY, I , _____ , have unconditional warm feelings for myself, my friends, and all I meet.

13. TODAY, I , _____ , am 100-percent alive, alert, and excited, because I abound in unlimited enthusiasm.

14. TODAY, I , _____ , am unusually confident, receiving an increasing amount of abundance.

15. TODAY, I , _____ , have replaced all negative thoughts with their opposite, positive thought.

16. TODAY, I , _____ , maintain control of my actions and emotions to achieve my greatness.

17. TODAY, I , _____ , live a life constantly enlarging as I seek beauty, joy, love, and peace.

18. TODAY, I , _____ , enjoy the beauty of fun, friendships, laughter, pleasure, and radiant joy.

19. TODAY, I , _____ , decide what thoughts will enter my mind and receive those I choose.

20. TODAY, I , _____ , release the true greatness within me as my self-appreciation expands.

21. TODAY, I , _____ , enrich my life as all my activity and conduct is results-oriented.

22. TODAY, I , _____ , am moving on to a higher level of fulfillment as my life unfolds.

23. TODAY, I , _____ , am energized by newfound purpose, goals, dreams, and dynamic excitement.

24. TODAY, I , _____ , believe and receive the unlimited prosperity that surrounds me.

25. TODAY, I , _____ , welcome the power of change and will ride the crest of opportunity.

26. TODAY, I , _____ , excitedly live this day in the beautiful unfolding of God's love.

No man can be happy unless he feels his life is in some way important.

27. TODAY, I , _____ , bless all mankind with my thoughts, prayers, and encouragement.
28. TODAY, I , _____ , look for, seek out, encourage, and recognize every sign of good in others.
29. TODAY, I , _____ , experience empathy, understanding, compassion, and love for all people.
30. TODAY, I , _____ , delight in the joyous feelings I receive and give to all my friends.
31. TODAY, I , _____ , love everyone unconditionally as a conduct of my love for myself.

Self-esteem is the package of beliefs you carry around in your head that you have accepted to be the truth about you whether it is or not.

The single greatest assurance that you have genuine self-esteem is, *Can you take total control of your mind?*

Pres. Abraham Lincoln's wife, Mary Todd, had deep-seated emotional problems. She spent money to excess, buying clothes she would never wear. Her greatest emotional outbursts were against the president. One night, she instructed President Lincoln to go to the grocery store the next morning to pick up some items. President Lincoln forgot and was conducting a Cabinet meeting at nine the next morning, when Mrs. Lincoln burst into the Cabinet room and cursed, blamed, and condemned the president because he didn't go to the grocery store, her punishment for him. He smilingly nodded his head during some fifteen minutes of her out-of-control tirade. When she ran down, he hugged her and said, "You are right, Mrs. Lincoln, you told me to go and I forgot it. I deserve what you have said." He turned to his secretary and asked her to send someone else to the store. He hugged Mrs. Lincoln again and ushered her out the door.

---

*"Our greatest glory is not in never falling,
but in rising every time we fall."*

Confucius

Then he returned to his seat at the head of the conference table, smiled and said that he was glad she had done that.

Secretary of War Steward asked President Lincoln what he meant by that, to which the president responded, "Why, Mr. Steward, she feels better now."

When you can take a tirade like that, overlook it, and forgive the person doing it, you are in control of your life and reveal your high self-esteem.

Causes of Low Self-Esteem

1. Negative body image
2. Critical blow-ups
3. Critical tapes; feelings of self-criticism you have accepted from others about yourself
4. Chronic comparisons to others that placed you in a lesser light
5. Demands of perfection imposed by others who also felt less than perfect
6. A sense of hopelessness
7. Inability to accept a compliment or to believe anything good can happen to you

Playing the If-Then Game

1. If I am nice, then people will like me.
2. If I am beautiful, then I will never be alone.
3. If I am smart, then I will be valued.
4. If I make people laugh, then no one will be angry with me.
5. If I am super-competent, then I will have many career opportunities.
6. If I lose weight, then everything in life will be fine.

"Losing isn't fatal and winning isn't final."

Don Shula

Sources of High Self-Esteem
(originally listed in chapter 2)

Parental approval. A child needs this from the first days of life and always after. This includes his own sense of personhood, his own sense of proven ability, his own sense of individuality, his own sense of realistic achievements, and meaningful values.

Other adult models. Relatives and friends of parents, as well as teachers, clergy, etc.

Siblings and peers. We become what the crowd we run with is.

Educational achievements.

Skills mastery. This includes mastery in sports, music, hobbies, games, etc.

Learning to feed ourselves good strokes.

Affirming romantic experiences. Being in love may be life's most exciting experience.

Receiving God's love. Religion that unloads guilt, fear, and blame without God's forgiveness may do serious damage to people's feelings about themselves.

Career expertise.

Root-value transfer. This necessary to receive strong feelings of belonging, respect, and the ability to identify with our forefathers.

What Every Human Being Needs

1. To belong, to be meaningfully involved in something that really counts.
2. To feel success in some achievement which he regards as his own thing.
3. To feel compassion, freedom, and discovery.
4. To be able to use his life to make a difference in his own world.

An affirmation is a positive thought that you consciously choose to immerse in your consciousness to produce a desired result.

5. To live comfortably in the face of constant anxiety.
6. To cope with threats against his identity—both real and imagined.
7. To feel genuine control over his own destiny, to create his own future.
8. To be responsible for his own behavior, to know the consequences of it, and to face the consequences with total acceptance.
9. To own a self-concept that is real, relevant, appropriate, and respected.
10. To have a number of chances to become a better person than he is right now and the freedom to want to.
11. To develop a capacity for sharing strong feelings of affection with at least one other person.
12. To be open to change and personal growth. To become an agent of constructive change in the world and to value the outcome, the process, and the traditions.
13. To have an ideology he can value and share.
14. To have a chance to learn as much as he can, as well as he can, and as fast as he can about what is true in the universe.
15. To have a will to try and a reason to want to.

We must build into every person the resources to face anything, not just to fill his tank, but to give him the techniques for manufacturing his own fuel, handling his own repairs, and perhaps building his own vehicle from his own resources in his own world—and then to make it in our shared world.

All human beings have the same basic needs. We strive in many ways to meet those needs and to satisfy our desires. Show people how they can achieve their own wants, needs, desires, and purposes through what you are doing.

You are the source of your own self-loving energy.
You now have an internal self-support system. You have
built a constructive program of self-care and self-nurturing.

Positive Quotes

Errors are evidence that you are human—and what's wrong with being human?—or better yet, a human becoming.

Good things usually begin with a difficulty, but great things invariably begin with an impossibility. Welcome the impossible as the messenger of impending greatness.

Most people allow their lives to be controlled by "they" and "luck." Why hand over your life to excuses or the whims of fortune? Remember: "they" is us, and "luck" is when preparation meets opportunity.

Are you playing it too safe? Success will come to you in direct proportion to the number of times you are willing to risk failure.

What do you stand for? What do you want your children to tell their children about you?

"The difference between perseverance and obstinacy is that one often comes from a strong will, and the other comes from a strong won't."   Henry Ward Beecher

You are completely responsible for all your responses to other persons and events. You control your response—and therein lies your freedom.

"Once your mind is stretched by a new idea, it will never again return to its original size."

Oliver Wendell Holmes

One definition of integrity: being on the "inside" what you profess to be the "outside."

You can't leave footprints in the sand of time by sitting on your butt, and who wants to leave buttprints in the sands of time?

"You think me the child of circumstances: I make my circumstances."
Ralph Waldo Emerson

God's easiest task is to make us humble, but his most difficult task is to make us positive.

Why not give teamwork a try? Put two people with a common goal together and suddenly, one plus one is more than two.

Whenever you undertake a new project, attempt to make as many mistakes as rapidly as possible in order to learn as much as you can in a short period of time.

Two weeks before he died, a young boy who had lived in a plastic bubble because of a rare disease, left that bubble for the very first time. He was able to kiss his mother . . . sleep on a real bed . . . walk barefoot on real grass. These simple things, which are all around us, gave him great joy.

The smallest goal achieved stands taller than the grandest intention. Do whatever your heart leads you to do—but do it. Don't beat up on yourself. Some of the worst "demotivators" in the English language are the words, "I should have . . . I would have . . . I could have." Why not make a conscious effort to strike them from your vocabulary? Instead, say to yourself, "Next time, I'll . . ."

You may occasionally give out, but never give up.

Purpose is the engine that powers your life.

"You will never find time for anything. If you want time, you must make it."   Charles Buxton

Gossip has no place in the thoughts or conversation of the successful person. It is just as harmful to the gossiper as it is to the person being gossiped about.

"Self-examination, if it is thorough enough, is nearly always the first step towards change—no one who learns to know

---

"Treat people as if they were what they ought to be and you help them to become what they are capable of being."
Goethe

himself remains just what he was before."

Thomas Mann

The energy derived from setting goals comes in large part from the focus it brings to our lives. It's like igniting a fire by channeling the gentle rays of the sun to a single spot through a magnifying glass.

Losers always have an excuse. Winners always have an idea.

Seen on a bumper sticker: "God loves you—whether you like it or not."

"No airplane was designed to taxi down the runway. They were all designed to fly high in the sky, above the clouds, above the storms. How many people do you know who spend their lives taxiing down the runways of life, revving their engines, but afraid to take off? We were all designed to fly."

Dr. H. Paul Jacobi

By intentionally raising your own expectations of yourself, you will create a gap between where you are and where you wish to be. Having created this gap for yourself, everything about you will automatically begin working on your behalf to close it. This explains why goal-setters enjoy boundless energy. Losers say, "Why don't they do something?" Winners say, "Here's something to do."

Most organizations are looking for ways to help people become better employees. High-performance organizations recognize that the key is finding ways to help employees become better people.

Though the road you're walking may be well-traveled, that does not necessarily mean it is leading to your destination.

"Each of us is connected to all living things whether we are aware of this beautiful fact or not. And, should you ever

"Enthusiasm is self-confidence in action."

Franklin Field

begin to feel that you are becoming separated from the world, you are simply self-deceived, for you could no more do this than a wave could separate itself from the ocean and still be a wave."   Gerald Jampolsky

In the Auschwitz death camp, a group of inmates told Victor Frankl that they no longer expected anything from life, but Frankl responded that they had it backward: "Life expects something of you, and it is up to every individual to discover what it should be."

You can never be completely successful as a whole person until you learn to be considerate of every person with whom you come into contact.

"One machine can do the work of fifty ordinary people. No machine can do the work of one extraordinary person."
                                              Elbert Hubbard

"With ordinary talent and extraordinary perseverance, all things are attainable."   Thomas F. Buxton

Personality can open many doors, but only character will keep them open.

If you don't feel good, act like you do, and you will almost immediately feel like you do. That's the way it works. Researchers have now determined that a smile—even if forced—triggers an intricate series of responses throughout the body, all of which conspire to make you feel good.

"A loss of courage may be the most striking feature which an outside observer notices in the West today."
                                      Alexander Solzhenitzyn

Historically, a decline in courage has signaled the beginning of the end. You are history in motion; your greatest power is your power to choose. Choose courageously.

Bad start? No sweat. It's the finish, not the start that counts.

I am a unique person reaching forth toward the fulfillment I deserve.

"No person was ever honored for what he received. Honor has been the reward for what he gave."

Pres. Calvin Coolidge

"Life is like playing the violin in public and learning the instrument as you go along."   Samuel Butler

Rather than acknowledge a mistake, nations have gone to war, families have separated, and individuals have sacrificed everything dear to them. Admitting that you have been wrong is just another way of saying that you are wiser today than yesterday. All meaningful and lasting change starts in the imagination and works its way down. Therefore, dream often . . . and dream big.

"Virtually all new ideas which have resulted in change in our society were at one time scorned (or illegal). . . . People ridiculed the Edisons, Henry Fords, Einsteins, and Wright Brothers—until they were successful."   Dr. Wayne Dyer

Predict another good day for yourself. Expect something great to happen.

Conclusion

Any time a negative thought enters your mind, contradict it with its opposite, positive thought.

Plan every day so that the conduct of that day's activity is under your mental and emotional control.

Saturate your thoughts with positive affirmations so that the conduct is obedient to the positive thought. Dr. Brach Waynbaum discovered in 1907, "Facial expression takes place before the brain acts to express that facial emotion." The thought precedes the emotion. Decide you will be happy, smile, and the brain responds accordingly. The smile sends an oxygen explosion to the brain.

"The secret of success is constancy of purpose."
Prime Minister Benjamin Disraeli

Look for every opportunity to serve other people. Dr. Albert A. Schweitzer once commented, "I don't know what your destiny will be, but I do know the only ones among you who will be truly happy will be those who have sought and found how to serve."

I am the best friend to myself. I take me out whenever I feel low. I alone am responsible for my feelings and I chose to feel beautiful.

CHAPTER 11

Guidelines for a Self-Celebrating Life

Retired Vice Adm. James Stockdale received our nation's highest medal for valor, the congressional Medal of Honor, for more than 200 combat missions and his leadership while a POW for eight years in North Vietnam. Now, professor of philosophy at Stanford University and author of several books, his own life provides a formula for others to live a courageous life:

1. Don't worry about things you don't control. People with high self-esteem take life's battles and problems without flinching and make the most out of each situation.
2. Courage is endurance in the presence of fear. Fear is a coward and flees the moment we face it.
3. You *are* your brother's keeper. No man is totally free while other men are enslaved. When we love and value ourselves, we love and value others.
4. Hatred and all other negative emotions are self-defeating. We replace negative emotions with their opposite, positive emotions.

Self-acceptance. People with high self-esteem honestly acknowledge all of their strengths and accept that any so-called weaknesses are areas that we haven't found time to confront and win over. Pride is "I have." Self-esteem is "I can."

Self-acceptance is self-value, self-commitment, and

self-confidence to face the fact that we are not perfect, but are growing, experiencing, and becoming all we desire to be. Self-acceptance is unconditional in that we admit our imperfections as areas we are improving. As we do grow, develop, and overcome, we develop more and more self-esteem.

People that do not now experience overwhelming self-esteem may be assured that they can do so by accepting themselves as of value, capable, worthy, and victorious. To accept ourselves means that this is where we are now, not where we are going to be. Life is a journey, not a destination. Because we are and have been achieving, we will continue on this adventure as long as we live and pursue self-esteem. The human brain, except for chemical imbalance or disease, is the only part of man that continues to defy age and senility. It expands and develops as long as we live.

We can develop self-acceptance by discarding the garbage and renewing the emotions. Try this exercise:

I discard fear and replace it with courage.
I discard ineptness and replace it with achievement.
I discard laziness and replace it with goals and life control.
I discard negative emotions and replace them with their opposite, positive emotions.
I discard guilt and replace it with good feelings about my personhood.
I discard depression and replace it with enthusiasm.
I discard inaction and replace it with controlled conduct.
I discard hatred and replace it with compassion.

Now discard other feelings and replace them.

_____

_____

"Freedom is the one thing you can't have unless you give it to others."
William Allen White

Self-interest vs. selfishness: do I exist for myself, for God, or for others? Auguste Comte, the nineteenth-century advocate of collectivism, coined a term, "altruism." Altruism holds that a human being must make the welfare of others his primary moral concern, placing their interests above his or her own sake.

Beneto Mussolini said, "Fascism . . . a life in which the individual, through the denial of himself, through the sacrifice of his own private interests, through death itself, realizes that complete spiritual existence in which his value as a man lies."

According to Joseph Goebbels, in *Escape From Freedom* by Erich Fromm: "To be a socialist is to submit the 'I' to the 'thou.'" Socialism is the sacrifice of the individual to the whole.

But the Bible teaches otherwise. As mentioned earlier, nineteen times in the Bible we are commanded to love ourselves. Paul writes, "So ought men to love their wives as their own bodies. He that loveth his wife loveth himself." (Eph. 5:28) And in explaining the two greatest commandments, Jesus says of the second: "And the second is like, namely this, 'Thou shalt love thy neighbour as thyself.' There is none other commandment greater than these." (Mark 12:31) In Matthew 5:13-16, Jesus tells his disciples:

> Ye are the salt of the earth: but if the salt have lost its savour, wherewith shall it be salted? It is thenceforth good for nothing, but to be cast out, and to be trodden under foot of men.

"It is a funny thing about life. If you refuse to accept anything but the best, you will get it."
Somerset Maugham

> Ye are the light of the world. A city that is set on a hill cannot be hid. Neither do men light a candle, and put it under a bushel, but on a candlestick; and it giveth light unto all that are in the house. Let your light so shine before men, that they may see your good works, and glorify your Father which is in heaven.

The Christian principle, then, is to be of value, salt so others may be saved. Salt keeps food from spoiling, and brings out the flavor, the best in it. Light is to shine to bring hope and to illuminate the darkness. It is not to burn out, but to continue to burn constantly and consistently for others to benefit from and find safe passage to safety.

Selfishness is "I'll get mine first and to hell with everyone else." Self-interest is "I will become whole, a light, a saving influence from degradation, from ruin so that others may also find the way to wholeness." Self-interest is primary. We can't help someone else if we are unable. We can't pull others from the deep waters if our own feet are not safely on shore. We can't love others if we don't love ourselves. We can't train and inspire others if we haven't been there ourselves. We can't show others how to cross the dangerous stream if we haven't discovered the safe rocks to step on. So, self-esteem is self-interest, so that the wholeness of our experiences can spill over and be shared with others coming our way.

Positive self-talk. You must be your own self-nurturing parent. If you are waiting for someone else to affirm you, and he doesn't, then you fall apart. Develop the interdependent attitude that you and you alone will affirm your self-worth.

Benjamin Franklin had a wonderful program of self-growth. Each year he wrote out the thirteen areas of his life that he wanted to improve, for example: saving, creativity,

---

"If you have your heart fixed on what you want,
there is nothing I can do to stop you from getting it."
Andrew Carnegie

human relations, industry, etc. Then he spent a full week on each of these. At the end of the first quarter he started over again. At the end of the year he had invested four weeks, a quarter apart, working on achieving these areas in his life. At the end of the year he started over again. If there was any conduct he felt he had not mastered, then he included that conduct in the next year. In this way, he took charge of his life and was one of the best informed, achieving people of his day or any day.

Now try this program for yourself. Remember, the only thing you control is your own mind. Do not surrender your mind, your emotions to others—only to God and yourself.

Begin each day with thoughtful meditation. Arise a half-hour early and invest this precious time in yourself. Read good books, the Bible, poetry, inspiring thoughts, and affirmations. When you dress, realize that you have ten coats in your closet. They are numbered from one to ten. One is the lowest, the despair coat. Ten is the highest, the self-esteem, the high-excitement coat. Decide which coat you are going to wear today. If you chose a "ten" coat, you will be in charge of your emotions all day. You will relate to other ten's and they will relate to you. The six's and seven's will climb higher by having experienced your ten conduct.

On entering your car, turn on your motivational audiotapes and play them all the way to the office and upon your return home. Turn your auto into a university. Play the tapes while you are dressing and before you go to sleep at night. Let every day be a growth day, a fulfilling day, and a learning day.

Live the twenty-one-day, goal-achieving experience. Find a quiet time, best early in the morning. Write out all the things you want to develop in your life: family achievement, personal growth, business success, spiritual fulfillment, etc. Then the next day, go over the previous day's goals and

---

Where there is hope, there are people. Where there are people, there is God. And where there is God, there is nothing missing.

write out goals for this day. Do this every day for twenty-one days and you will be amazed how effectively you have taken charge of your life.

Visualization: Jack Nicklaus, the greatest golfer of all time, sees, in his mind, the ball going exactly where he wants it to go. Then his muscles obey his mind. Visualize what you want to become. See your children (as I did) crossing the stage to receive their graduate degrees. See yourself accepting the awards of your associates, see yourself and your name on the door, as president of your company. See yourself accepting God's blessing, approval, and reward.

Self-Expectancy. The perfectionist is under a compulsive drive to do, but with no satisfaction. The person with low self-esteem has no expectancy because he/she has had all expectancy destroyed by criticism, fear, and self-doubt. The person with high self-esteem is the only one capable of defining and achieving self-expectancy and this will vary greatly.

Twenty-seven percent of the people in the nation expect something for nothing.

David McClellan, professor of psychology at Harvard University, reported after a thirty-five-year study that only sixty percent are just making it through.

Ten percent have goals to do, to accomplish. They are winners. They expect good things for themselves.

Three percent have goals to be. They are the super-winners. They 1) love problems to solve, 2) take reasonable risks, and 3) are committed to become all they are capable of becoming.

So it is with readers of this book:

Twenty percent will buy the book and never read it or finish it.

"Reading is to the mind what excellence is to the body."
Sir Richard Steele

Sixty percent will read it, find some inspiration from it, and get a general understanding of what high self-esteem is.

Twenty percent will read it, love it, read it again and again (you must read a book six times to get fifty percent of the value, and twenty times to get ninety percent of the value of a book), fill out the outlines, fill in the blanks, continue to get and stay excited, draw inspiration from it, and make a commitment to themselves to become all they are capable of becoming. *That's the best definition of self-expectancy.*

The Plan of Action for My Life

What

I want approval from _____ .
I want approval for _____ .
I want deeper bonding with my mate.
I want friends to listen and understand me better.
I want better-defined goals for myself, my team members at
    work, and my family members.
I want recognition for my achievement, promotions at work,
    and at home.
I want satisfying sexual experiences.
I want exhilarating peak experiences, emotionally, mentally,
    and spiritually.
I want variety, travel, exciting vacations and weekends, and
    renewing leisure.
I want forgiveness, guilt-free feelings, and a personal rela-
    tionship with God.
I want time to play, have fun, to rest, to renew, and to be
    constantly growing.
I want _____ .
I want _____ .
I want _____ .
I want _____ .

Just as the constant dripping of water will wear away the hardest
granite, so continued effort will overcome every obstacle.

I want _____ .

Who

I want approval, acceptance, and understanding from my parents.

I want approval, acceptance, and understanding from my mate and children.

I want approval, acceptance, and understanding from my team members and contemporaries.

I want approval, acceptance, and understanding from my clients and/or business associates.

I want approval, acceptance, and understanding from God and religious leaders.

I want approval, acceptance, and understanding from ____
_____ .

I want approval, acceptance, and understanding from ____
_____ .

I want approval, acceptance, and understanding from ____
_____ .

Myself

I want to really know all I can know about myself.

I want to understand how I have effectively dealt with the troubled past in my life.

I want to clearly plot my journey for a satisfying, achieving life.

I want to become all I can be.

I want _____ .

I want _____ .

I want _____ .

I want _____ .

Bucky Wertz was a 5-foot, 6-inch "walk-on" as a linebacker for the football team at Ohio State University in the fall of

The length of my life is influenced by how I take care of myself.

1946. The coach was shocked. He was too small. They would kill him, and he told Bucky so. At the end of practice, he told Bucky he couldn't play. The next day, Bucky was back in uniform. Coach called him over and said, "I told you I had cut you from the squad. You are too small; these guys will kill you." With a firm, committed voice, Bucky said, "Coach, with due respect, you nor no one else can prevent me from playing football for my school." The coach was shocked. He allowed Bucky to stay on the squad.

Bucky was the best tackler on the squad. Fast as lightning, sure on his feet, he would burst through the line and hit the ballcarrier before he could get started. Still, he was too small, the coaches agreed.

In the third game of the season, after the game was "in the bag," the coach sent Bucky in. He made every tackle the rest of the game. He started every game for the rest of the season and led the team in tackles.

The next season, Bucky was 5-feet, 8-inches, weighed in at 168 pounds, and led the team in tackles. Every season, junior and senior years, was the same.

On January 1, 1950, Ohio State played USC in the Rose Bowl. USC had an all-American fullback, weighing 240 pounds, who was the finest running back in the nation. Bucky was assigned to "rover" this fullback. The fullback never gained a yard. Bucky hit him behind the line every time he had the ball. Ohio State won in a shocking upset. Bucky Wertz had high self-esteem.

Now, test your own self-esteem (choose A or B):

1. A. I feel hurt when people disapprove of me.
   B. When criticized, I feel compassion for that person.

2. A. I control myself, my feelings, and my conduct.

---

*"The quality of a person's life is directly proportionate
to his/her commitment to excellence."*
Vince Lombardi

   B. When I feel out of control of myself and of others, I feel I'm "out of it."

3. A. I believe that I am no better or worse than other people.
   B. Since I'm an achiever, I feel I'm better than those who are not.

4. A. How I look at others is very important for I want to be admired.
   B. How I look is important, for it reflects how I feel about myself. I stay in shape always.

5. A. I don't pick arguments, but when they occur, I apply the win-win principle . . .
   B. I dislike arguments and seek to avoid them whenever I can.

6. A. It's very difficult for me to turn down an opportunity to help someone.
   B. I help others when I can, but not at my own expense; I can say no when it's wise.

7. A. I do my best always, because I enjoy life that way.
   B. It pains me when I don't do my best, because that is what everyone should do.

8. A. I detest making mistakes and avoid them whenever I can.
   B. I don't enjoy making mistakes, but they don't bother me. I learn from them.

9. A. Whenever I need help, I ask for it from whoever can help me.

"Enthusiasm is not merely an outward expression.
It works from within. Enthusiasm is born of genuine liking
for some phase of what you are doing."
Anonymous

B. I do not like to ask for help. I should be able to do it myself.

10. A. When others do things wrong, I tell them so. Then I feel better.
    B. I am not critical of others. They don't learn from criticism; they learn from examples.

11. A. When others differ with me, I listen; that's their right, and I learn.
    B. When others differ with me, I set them straight. I like to help people do it right.

12. A. I don't like to be praised. It makes me feel uneasy.
    B. When I receive praise, that's nice, but I don't have to have it.

13. A. If people like me, that's nice, but not necessary. I like myself.
    B. I like to make new friends. They are very important and meaningful to me.

14. A. Achieving my best is very important to me, and I want it.
    B. Success, wealth, and recognition come to me as a net result of my own high self-esteem.

15. A. Life is so enjoyable and fulfilling that I seldom take time to look back.
    B. I tell others about my successes because that makes me feel good and may help them.

16. A. When mistakes occur, it usually is the fault of someone else.
    B. I take full responsibility for my mistakes. Blaming others does no good.

17. A. My achievement is the result of who I am, not the

"The best effect of any book is that it excites the reader to self activity."
Thomas Carlyle

goals I have set.

B. I set goals and strive to reach them. Then I know someday I will have it all.

18. A. I can be outspoken when necessary. Others need to get things right.

B. My happiness means I can speak my opinions without being harsh to others.

19. A. Others do what is in their best interests, right or wrong.

B. I really get upset when people are treated unfairly and let others know it.

20. A. I watch carefully what I say, because I don't want to be hurt back.

B. I will not let others' words hurt me. It's what I say to myself that counts.

Answers are at the end of the chapter.

Affirmations

1. Every day, in every way, I am getting better.
2. I am constantly moving onto a higher level of fulfillment and consciousness as my life unfolds.
3. I delight in the joyous feelings I share with dear friends.
4. No one can make me stoop so low as to hate him.
5. I learn something useful and meaningful from every person I meet.
6. I share, love, trust, support, and encourage all people, especially my children.
7. I am patient, tender, and understanding in dealing with all people.
8. Since I accept myself unconditionally, I find others accept me the same.

Talent is God's gift to you. What you do with it is your gift to God.

9. People will respond positively to me, because my personality is controlled by my positive mental attitude.

10. I seek to become more charming, persuasive, and popular every day I live.

11. I draw people to me by the power of my love for them.

12. I will not be an emotional cripple controlled by negative attitudes.

13. I relate to positive-minded people and choose not to expose my sensitive emotions to negative-minded people, because such thoughts are destructive.

14. I dwell on beautiful, powerful thoughts of self-affirmation.

15. My personality is the outward expression of the inward person, and I want that person to be fulfilling and whole so I will be well-received.

16. The happiest people are those with achieving experiences of helping others.

17. I can develop the skill of getting along with people.

18. I can cure many of my own ills by helping a friend cure his.

19. "If thou canst believe, all things are possible to them that believeth." (Mark 9:23)

20. "For as he thinketh in his heart, so is he. . . ." (Prov. 23:7)

21. God is my instant, constant, and abundant source of energy, love, and peace.

22. "And all things, whatsoever ye shall ask in prayer, believing, ye shall receive." (Matt. 21:22)

23. The love of God lives in me, the peace of God lives as me, the power of God flows through me; wherever I am, God is, and all is well.

24. Success is the persistent achievement of a worthy, challenging goal.

"Most people are about as happy as they make up their mind to be."
Pres. Abraham Lincoln

25. Success is the reward you give yourself for having the courage to do with your life what you want to do and doing it well.
26. The greatest use of life is to so live your life that the use of your life outlives your life.
27. Every misfortune always carries the seed of an equal or greater benefit.
28. Not failure, but low aim is the real crime in life.
29. Our life is what our thoughts make us.
30. I can change my life by changing my attitudes or my mind.
31. When I have felt depressed or discouraged, it is because of the ways I have let myself think and act.

In 1968, I was in Belem, Brazil, on the Amazon River. A friend, Glen Goble, arranged to take me to visit the national leper colony, some twenty miles from the city.

Some eight hundred lepers from all over the nation live there, families in their own cottages, raising their children, the vast majority never contaminated by the disease. Upon finishing high school in the colony, they are sent forth to work or college, leaving their parents in the colony. The mayor, Jose, is also pastor of the Baptist church in the colony. He took us on a tour of the colony, visiting the hospital where those in the final stages of this dread disease live out their final days under medication and care.

Then we went to Jose's modest two-bedroom home. We met Maria, a beautiful, lovely lady, now nearly fifty years old, giving a piano lesson to a twelve-year-old girl. Maria had a cloth covering her arms, because her hands had dropped off with leprosy.

At thirteen years of age, Maria had gone with her mother

"If one advances confidently in the direction of his dreams and endeavors, to live the life which he has imagined, he will meet with success unexpected in common people."
Henry D. Thoreau

to Paris, France, to study ballet and the organ. She was the most outstanding ballerina and organist in all of Brazil. For three years, she studied in Paris and was the rage of Europe in both dance and music.

Then she returned to Brazil for the summer. She came down with leprosy. The disease was no respecter of her talents, or the fact that her father was one of the wealthiest men in Brazil. The law required that she be placed in a leper colony. Can you imagine a more shocking experience? Jose, a poor worker's son, had been sent to the colony at age eighteen. He fell in love with Maria, and she responded to this handsome and kind man.

At age nineteen, Jose's leprosy was arrested, and he was released from the colony. He spent a year away, pining for Maria. Then, he went back to the colony as a government employee, to invest his life there with Maria. They were married, he free of the disease, she not. He studied to become the pastor, and at age forty, became the mayor and chief government employee in the colony.

Maria taught hundreds of children piano, organ, and ballet. She sent forth some of the most talented students in all Brazil, filled with the love and dedication Maria gave them.

I have never experienced such love, devotion, and such a happy home like Maria and Jose shared. They both have high self-esteem, giving their lives for others. Some years later, Maria died of leprosy, leaving Jose to carry on and leaving a heritage of love and devotion seldom seen.

Answers to Self-Esteem Test: 1-A, 2-B, 3-A, 4-B, 5-A, 6-B, 7-A, 8-B, 9-A, 10-B, 11-A, 12-B, 13-A, 14-B, 15-A, 16-B, 17-A, 18-B, 19-A, 20-B.

If you had 16—20 right, you have an outstanding sense of high self-esteem.

Share success, love, appreciation, and unconditional love and acceptance with all members of your family.

12—15 means you are on your way to having high self-esteem.

If you scored lower than this, you need a lot of work!

Conclusion

The only thing you and I totally control is our own minds. Determine that you will never surrender your high self-esteem to other people's negative thoughts about you.

Live in a day-by-day high of self-celebration.

Plan your joy time and luxuriate in it.

Be the best friend to yourself. Take yourself out to experience meaningful, free-from-regret pleasures that enhance your self.

Make your job a joyous, achieving event every day.

Give more of yourself in personal and family relationships than you expect to receive.

Live the ideal of "I will live my life so that the use of my life will outlive my life."

Blackie was from the Hell's Kitchen section of New York City. He carried a heavy load of self-hate that reflected itself in his spending several months in the brig.

Blackie was the worst marine in training I ever saw. Blackie was the greatest marine in combat I ever saw. He was so outstanding that our colonel said this to a new lieutenant just assigned to the platoon Blackie was in during combat in Okinawa: "Lieutenant, if I had the power, I would place you under the command of this private, Blackie. He's the most brilliant combat marine I've ever seen. Listen to him. He'll keep you alive."

Two days later, Blackie was dead. I helped bring his body in. He had been hit on the left wrist, shattering the bone, penetrating his watch and going into his chest. The doctor

*"Pray as if everything depended upon God and work
as if everything depended upon man."*
Cardinal Francis J. Spellman

said, "Look at this." He picked the bullet out of Blackie's chest with this fingers. It had barely punctured his skin, not even entering the muscle or bone. "These hits are not life-threatening. He died of shock. He expected to die. It was self-induced."

In 1961, I was driving a new Chrysler on a two-lane high-way in Mississippi when a car came out from my left, failed to see me, and hit my car on the side, flipping me. I was trav-eling seventy-five miles an hour and had no time to avoid being hit. My car turned over ten times in a water-filled ca-nal before coming to a stop, upside down, some distance down the road. The top of the car was level with the dash-board, all four wheels were gone. I touched my seat belts, opened the door (other doors had to be opened later with a blow torch), and swam to shore. I couldn't see out of my left eye, and my face was covered with blood. I walked back some distance to the road where I was hit, having covered my left eye with my handkerchief. A Mr. Bell met me there, removed my handkerchief, and said, "Your eye is not in-jured, you have a cut on your forehead. I'll take you to the hospital."

We got into his pickup truck and started into town. I be-gan to use self-hypnosis on myself to control the pain in my head. By the time we had driven the four miles into town, I felt no pain. I had a considerable cut on my head that took a number of stitches.

The doctor said, "Why aren't you in shock? I've seen peo-ple die of shock with less injuries than you."

I told him about Blackie and said, "My high self-esteem has given me the confidence to overcome problems, not to be overcome by problems."

The three most important words in communication:
"You are important."

Blackie died because of low self-esteem. I lived because of high self-esteem.

The California Task Force found self-esteem was "appreciating my own worth and importance and having the character to be accountable for myself and to act responsibly toward others." Dr. John Talbert, professor and chairman of the department of psychiatry at the University of Maryland School of Medicine, says that self-esteem is often the result of a combination of factors: early childhood events, genetics, and personality. "It's the sum total of experiences, thoughts, fears, and fantasies that come together in a composite impression of how we are."

Martin E. Ford, a developmental and educational psychologist at Stanford University who has studied self-esteem for more than a decade, believes "it's an evaluation that things are going well with you."

So, there is no short cut to high self-esteem. If you were bestowed self-esteem by your parents, teachers, and life experiences, consider yourself fortunate. If you were not so blessed, then determine that for the rest of your life you will pursue this highest of life's values, believing in yourself. Take charge of your life by using this workbook to certify your importance, to achieve high self-esteem.

"The greatest discovery of my generation is that human beings can alter their lives by altering their attitudes of mind."
William James

Bibliography

Benson, Herbert, and Klipper, Miriam Z. *The Relaxation Response.* New York: Avon, 1976.

Bone, Diane. *The Business of Listening.* Los Altos, CA: Crisp, 1988.

Branden, Nathaniel. *Honoring the Self: Personal Integrity and the Heroic Potentials of Human Nature.* Los Angeles: J. P. Tarcher, 1984.

_____. *How to Raise Your Self-Esteem.* New York: Bantam, 1988.

_____. *The Psychology of Self-Esteem.* New York: Bantam, 1971.

Briggs, Dorothy C. *Your Child's Self-Esteem: The Key to His Life.* New York: Doubleday, 1975.

Cousins, Norman. *Anatomy of an Illness As Perceived by the Patient.* New York: Bantam, 1983.

_____. *The Healing Heart.* New York: Avon, 1984.

Dell, Twyla. *An Honest Day's Work: Motivating Employees to Give Their Best.* Los Altos, CA: Crisp, 1988.

Douglas, Mack R. *Freedom Unlimited.* West Palm Beach, FL: Easy Read Publishing Co., 1983.

_____. *How to Give Your Child Self-Esteem.* West Palm Beach, FL: Easy Read Publishing Co., 1986.

_____. *How to Make a Habit of Succeeding.* Grand Rapids, MI: Zondervan, 1987.

_____. *How to Raise Drug-Free Children.* West Palm Beach, FL: Easy Read Publishing Co., 1986.

Farrell, Warren. *The Liberated Man.* New York: Random House, 1974.

Felleman, Hazel, ed., *Best Loved Poems of the American People.* New York: Doubleday, 1936.

Hanson, Peter G. *The Joy of Stress.* New York: Doubleday, 1985.

_____. *Stress for Success.* New York: Ballentine, 1990.

Hart, Louise. *The Winning Family: Increasing Self-Esteem in Your Children and Yourself.* New York: Lifeskills Press, 1989.

207

Iocacca, Lee. *Talking Straight*. New York: Bantam, 1984.

Lozanov, Georgi. *Suggestology and Outlines of Suggestopedy*. New York: Gordon & Breach, 1978.

Porat, Freida. *Self-Esteem: The Key to Success in Work and Love*. Saratoga, CA: R & E Publishers, 1982.

Ray, Sondra. *I Deserve Love*. Berkeley, CA: Celestial Arts, 1987.

Satir, Virginia. *Self-Esteem*. Berkeley, CA: Celestial Arts, 1975.

Siegel, Bernie. *Love, Medicine and Miracles*. New York: HarperCollins, 1986.

Waitley, Denis. *The Double Win*. New York: Berkley, 1986.

_____. *The Psychology of Winning*. New York: Berkley, 1984.

_____. *The Seeds of Greatness: The Ten Best Kept Secrets of Total Success*. New York: Picket, 1988.

_____. *The Winner's Edge*. New York: Berkley, 1984.

Waitley, Denis, and Witt, Reni. *The Joy of Working: The Thirty Day System to Success, Wealth and Happiness on the Job*. New York: Ballantine, 1986.